Fort Worth & Tarrant County:
An Historical Guide

Fort Worth & Tarrant County
An Historical Guide

Edited and revised by Carol Roark

A project of the Tarrant County Historical Society, Inc.

Texas Christian University Press
Fort Worth

Copyright © 2003 by Tarrant County Historical Society, Inc.

Library of Congress Cataloging-in-Publication Data

Fort Worth and Tarrant County : an historical guide / edited and revised
   by Carol Roark.
       p. cm.
"Copyright Tarrant County Historical Society"—T.p. verso.
Includes index.
   ISBN 0-87565-279-4 (alk. paper)
   1. Fort Worth (Tex.)—Tours. 2. Tarrant County (Tex.)—Tours. 3.
Historic buildings—Texas—Fort Worth—Guidebooks. 4. Historic
buildings—Texas—Tarrant County—Guidebooks. 5. Historic
sites—Texas—Tarrant County—Guidebooks. 6. Historic
sites—Texas—Fort Worth—Guidebooks. 7. Fort Worth (Tex.)—Buildings,
structures, etc.—Guidebooks. 8. Fort Worth (Tex.)—History. 9.
Tarrant County (Tex.)—History. I. Roark, Carol E. II. Tarrant County
Historical Society.
   F394.F7 F595 2003
   976.4'531—dc22
                                    2003017327

Design/illustrations by Shadetree Studio

Printed in Canada

In memory of
Josephine Terrell Smith Hudson

Table of Contents

Where the West Begins	2
Tarrant County History Timeline	10
Tarrant County Map	16
How to Use this Book	17
List of Area Maps	18
Definition of Terms	19
Fort Worth – Downtown	23
Courthouse and Sundance Square	24
Near Northeast	32
Mid-town	35
Water Garden Area	39
Fort Worth – North Side	47
Fort Worth – South Side	63
Fort Worth – West Side	79
Fort Worth Northeast and East Side	91
Southeast Tarrant County	105
Arlington	105
Mansfield	113
Northeast Tarrant County	119
Colleyville	119
Grapevine	119
Bedford	126
West Tarrant County	131
Westworth Village	131
Westover Hills	132
Cemeteries	137
Thematic Tours	157
African-American History	158
Cattle and Livestock Industry	159
Early Tarrant County History	160
Historic Residential Neighborhoods	161
Jewish History	162
Railroad History	163
Acknowledgements	165
Index	169

Where the West Begins

Where the West Begins

Fort Worth and Tarrant County were founded on a dividing line. East of the line, the land was fair game for American settlers. West of the line, the land was reserved for nomadic Indian tribes that had hunted, fished, and camped in this area for generations. The Treaty of Bird's Fort negotiated in August 1843 by General Edward H. Tarrant established the line. It was a delicate balancing act and one not destined to remain stable for long. In 1853, only five years after Major Ripley A. Arnold established Fort Worth on behalf of the U. S. Army, the military closed the fort, pulled up stakes, and moved to a new series of forts lying farther west.

Yet the 1849 to 1853 period when Fort Worth was, "where the West begins," has shaped the region's spirit and approach to life for more than a century and a half. After the fort closed, settlers who had clustered around the leaky palisade buildings on the bluff overlooking the Trinity River used the structures for their businesses. Other small communities scattered throughout the county found that as the line of settlement moved west, their settlements did not need the protection that the fort offered. Several – Birdville, Johnson Station, Grapevine, and the community that would become Azle – were easily as prosperous as the tiny community lodged in the old fort buildings.

Pushing the line of settlement farther west made Tarrant County a safe place to settle, and more people moved to the area to farm. In an 1856 election marked by the liberal distribution of free whiskey, Fort Worth won the county seat from Birdville and secured its future. Before the Civil War, the county had a few large slave-holding plantations and many small family farms. The eastern half of the county was more heavily populated than the western half. To the east, the land was part of the Eastern Cross Timbers with rolling plains, oak trees, and land suitable for agriculture; to the west lay the beginning of the Grand Prairie, with soils that supported grasslands more appropriate for ranching.

As with many southern communities, the Civil War had a dramatic impact on Tarrant County. Many families sent their sons to fight with the Confederacy, although there were a few Union sympathizers who opposed secession and the war. There were no battles fought in Tarrant County, but the Civil War consumed many of Tarrant County's resources and people. The county's population fell for the first time since it was established, from 6,020 people in 1860 to 5,788 in 1870.

As Texas struggled to rebuild its economy after the Civil War, entrepreneurs began to tap an unexpected source of income – the cattle that roamed the plains of South and West Texas. People in the northeastern states were hungry for beef, and Texans provided it by driving the cattle up long trails into Kansas where the animals were loaded onto rail cars and shipped east.

Fort Worth became an important stop on the cattle trail, a place to restock supplies, have a meal and a stiff drink, and – perhaps – enjoy the company of a working woman. The cowboys not only provided a boost for the local economy, they also helped make Fort Worth's reputation as a wide-open, anything-goes town.

Cattle and the cowboys who herded them through town brought money, but Fort Worth's place on the map wasn't assured until the first railroad line arrived in 1876. It wasn't an easy process. When the United States economy crashed following the Panic of 1873, the Texas & Pacific Railway stopped construction just west of Dallas. For three years Fort Worth's fate hung in the balance. People who had come to Fort Worth anticipating the arrival of the railroad moved away. One former resident, who had gone to Dallas, wrote an article in the Dallas paper saying that Fort Worth was such a sleepy little place that a panther could sleep undisturbed in the middle of Main Street. Fort Worth residents embraced the supposed insult and dubbed the community "Panther City." Finally, as a deadline for completion of the line to Fort Worth loomed, local citizens assisted the T & P in laying track, and the railroad finally steamed into town on July 19, 1876.

The arrival of the railroad dramatically changed the way of life not only for people in Fort Worth, but also for those living throughout the county. Building materials, home furnishings, manufactured goods, and other basics of civilized life could now be shipped less expensively via rail rather than hauled in by horse and wagon. Ranchers could now ship their livestock by rail from Fort Worth rather than enduring the long trail drives. For residents in the small towns scattered throughout the county, Fort Worth became "the big city" where stores carried an increasingly wide variety of goods. By 1887, Fort Worth had sixteen thousand inhabitants compared to Grapevine's eight hundred, Arlington's six hundred, and Mansfield's five hundred residents. With the cash infusion brought by the railroad, Fort Worth began to tear down its wood-frame frontier-town structures and rebuild in brick.

Within seventeen years, eight railroad lines came through Fort Worth, making it a transportation crossroads. B. B. Paddock, the newspaper editor and civic promoter, saw his 1873 prediction of a "tarantula map" – where Fort Worth was the body of the spider and the rail lines the legs – had finally come true. During the 1880s, railroads also arrived in other towns in Tarrant County that were not on the original Texas & Pacific route. Rail connections opened markets for agricultural goods, and the number of farms grew. Between 1890 and 1900, almost a thousand new farms were reported in Tarrant County. The principal crops produced were cotton, corn, and wheat. Regional centers such as Grapevine and Mansfield prospered during this period, as did the thriving farms that surrounded them.

In Fort Worth, civic leaders considered strategies to make more money from the cattle industry. Texas ranchers now brought cattle to Fort Worth and loaded them on rail cars for shipment to stockyards in the North and East. Some of the eastern markets complained about the ticks on Texas cattle and refused to accept them. Fort Worth leaders reasoned that if cattle could be slaughtered and processed in Fort Worth and the carcasses shipped via rail, the tick problem would be eliminated, and Fort Worth could claim more money from each cow that passed through the city. The lack of dependable refrigerated railcars proved a major stumbling block, however, and nineteenth-century efforts to establish a stockyards and meatpacking plant were not successful.

Finally, in 1902, local leaders found the answer they needed by partnering with two Chicago meatpacking giants, the Armour and Swift companies. Enticed by free land on the North Side, the two companies built plants to slaughter both cattle and hogs, and the Union Stockyards Company set up facilities to handle the sale of those animals as well as sheep, horses, and mules. By 1909, the packing plants were processing five thousand hogs and three thousand cattle daily. Employment opportunities in the packing plants brought significant numbers of ethnic minorities to the Fort Worth area for the first time. In addition to African American workers, the Armour and Swift plants hired many immigrants from central and eastern Europe as well as a number of Greeks to work in the slaughterhouses, and most lived in neighborhoods near their jobs. Fort Worth annexed North Fort Worth in 1909 and the stockyards and packing plants in 1923, bringing those important economic resources under the city's control.

Shortly after the turn of the century, the oil industry joined Fort Worth's livestock operations as a major economic force. Petroleum became important as a fuel source, but other commercial applications as a lubricant, as a component in manufactured products such as paint and detergent, and as an ingredient used in the production of plastics also helped create a strong market for Texas oil. Oil wells in fields in Electra, Burkburnett, Ranger, Desdemona, and Breckenridge pumped millions of barrels of oil per year. Fort Worth became a significant refining center when Gulf Oil opened a refinery in 1911, followed by Pierce Oil in 1912, and Magnolia Petroleum in 1914. Oil companies also located their business operations here, and many oilmen chose to make their "city" home in Fort Worth.

During the teens, the aviation and defense industries also got their start in Tarrant County. Aviation was in its infancy, but the European powers fighting in World War I knew that their pilots needed training to make the use of airplanes effective. The good, year-round flying weather in Texas was extremely attractive. Before the United States entered the war, Canadian and British pilots trained at three Tarrant County airfields: Hicks in northwestern Tarrant County near Saginaw, Benbrook or Carruthers in Benbrook, and Barron in Everman – also referred to as Taliaferro #1, #2 and #3 at one time. American pilots trained at these fields later in the war. The United States Army also had a presence in Tarrant County when Camp Bowie opened in 1917 to train the 36th Infantry Division. This huge facility covered over two thousand acres in the area that today is Fort Worth's historic West Side, and the trench system and rifle range in the western part of the camp were actually located in Benbrook. After the military closed Camp Bowie, the area was quickly developed for residential use. Camp Bowie Boulevard west of Montgomery Street runs through the area where the camp was located.

Tarrant County thrived during the 1920s. Farms and ranches throughout the outlying areas of the county flourished, as more sophisticated farm equipment and electricity made rural life easier. Fort Worth continued to enjoy the benefits of the oil boom. Successful businessmen built large homes in restricted subdivisions like Ryan Place, Monticello, and Rivercrest, and the Fort Worth Cats dominated Texas League baseball. Swank new hotels, including the Hotel Texas and the Blackstone, were built. Meacham Field, Fort Worth's airport, opened in 1927, providing yet another mode of transportation for people and goods. These early aviation efforts foreshadowed the decline of rail transportation and the rise of aviation that would occur following World War II.

However, the stock market crash of 1929 and the ensuing Great Depression proved to be a stumbling block in Tarrant County's progress. Although the still-thriving petroleum industry and several construction projects already underway helped bolster the economy through 1930, by 1931 the situation had begun to deteriorate. Throughout the county, farm prices fell, drought hurt crop yields, and farm foreclosures increased. In Fort Worth, unemployment began to rise despite stopgap programs to hire part-time laborers. Federal work relief programs, part of Franklin Roosevelt's New Deal, finally helped put substantial numbers of unemployed people back to work.

The Civilian Conservation Corps built several shelters and picnic tables at several parks around Lake Worth between 1934 and 1937, while the Public Works Administration constructed schools in Colleyville, Hurst, Azle, Saginaw, and Fort Worth, built a rock gymnasium in Mansfield, and enlarged the existing school in Everman. Other projects included a number of bridges built throughout the county, Farrington Field and the Will Rogers Memorial Coliseum and Auditorium in Fort Worth, and the recreation center in Keller. By 1941, the federal government had spent more than $15 million locally to combat the effects of the Great Depression.

The Fort Worth Frontier Centennial, held in 1936 to celebrate the centennial of Texas independence, also pumped dollars into the local economy. The exposition grounds were located in what is today's Cultural District, on the southwest corner of University Drive and Lancaster Avenue. Although the state's main celebration was held in Dallas, civic promoter and newspaper publisher Amon G. Carter made sure that visitors knew that they should "go to Dallas for education [but] come to Fort Worth for entertainment."

World War II and a fistful of government defense contracts brought an end to the Great Depression in Tarrant County and began an era in which the aviation industry fueled its economic growth. In addition to the Consolidated Vultee Aircraft Corporation's "bomber plant" on Fort Worth's West Side, Globe Aircraft Corporation opened a plant in Saginaw that built training planes for the army. By the end of World War II, Consolidated Vultee (now Lockheed Martin) employed thirty-five thousand workers, and Carswell Air Force Base next door was home to the Strategic Air Command. Bell Helicopter moved to Tarrant County in 1951. It first occupied the old Globe Aircraft plant in Saginaw but moved to a new facility in Hurst in 1970. Defense industry work brought many families to Tarrant County during the 1950s and 1960s. The county's population grew from 361,253 in 1950 to 538,495 in 1960, an increase of sixty-seven percent.

With this increase in population, Tarrant County's rural communities also began to change. Towns that had once been rural farming centers became suburban bedroom communities, from which many commuters made their way into Fort Worth or Dallas to work. Arlington's population also began to increase rapidly after the General Motors Assembly Plant opened in 1951, creating jobs for the many skilled workers who moved into Arlington and surrounding communities. With this increased traffic came the need for better highways. The main Fort Worth freeways, East-West (Interstate 30) and North-South (United States Highway 81; Interstate 35W) were built during the early 1950s, and the Dallas-Fort Worth Turnpike (now the portion of Interstate 30 running between Fort Worth and Dallas) opened in 1957. Several state highways connecting more rural parts of the county were either built or expanded during this time period, but travel to and from some of these communities was still slow.

Both Fort Worth and Dallas also recognized the need for a better airport, but both also wanted the facility located close to their city. Initial construction on a project called "Midway Airport" began in 1942, but there was a disagreement between Dallas and Fort Worth about which way the terminal should face. Dallas continued to put its efforts into Love Field, so Fort Worth annexed the Midway site and renamed it Amon G. Carter Field.

In 1960, the airport was renamed Greater Southwest International Airport and an attempt made to operate it as an airfield serving both Fort Worth and Dallas. With Love Field still active, Dallas residents declined to drive further west to the regional airport, and the number of flights out of the field declined. In 1964 the Civil Aeronautics Board told Dallas and Fort Worth leaders that they had 180 days to come up with a location for a new regional airport. A mediator helped the two cities reach agreement, and a parcel of land straddling the county line just north and east of the older failed airport was selected. Construction began in 1968, and the world's fourth largest airport, now Dallas-Fort Worth International Airport, opened in January of 1974.

The 1980s saw tremendous growth throughout Tarrant County. Fort Worth grew more slowly than the suburban communities, but the entire county's economy diversified as DFW Airport linked Tarrant County with the world at large. Fort Worth Alliance Airport joined the aviation industry, already anchored by American Airlines, Lockheed Martin Corporation, and Bell Helicopter Textron, Inc., when the industrial airport opened in 1989. Electronics giant Radio Shack, headquartered in Fort Worth, is a major employer, as is the cellular telephone company, Nokia, with a factory located at Alliance Airport. The medical industry employs thousands in Tarrant County through Harris Methodist Hospitals, the Cook Children's Medical Center, and the health products manufacturer, Alcon Laboratories, Inc. There is even still a railroad presence in Tarrant County, although the Burlington Northern Santa Fe Railway represents a merger of several lines that once operated here.

Despite all this growth, Fort Worth and Tarrant County have cherished their heritage. There is an old joke that says, "If Fort Worth is where the West begins, then Dallas must be where the East peters out." While

Dallas has seemed intent on always building something newer, bigger, and better, Fort Worth and Tarrant County have successfully blended heritage with economic growth. Despite pressures, historic preservation has played a vital role in protecting the significant buildings and sites that tell the stories of the people who created the history of this county. Wander through Sundance Square in Fort Worth, ride the train between the Fort Worth Stockyards and Grapevine's historic train depot, marvel at the pioneer cabins at Log Cabin Village and the Middleton Tate Johnson Plantation Cemetery and Park, and walk through the streets of our historic neighborhoods. We invite you to enjoy the charm that this unique blend of history and progress has to offer.

Tarrant County History Timeline

1841 Jonathan Bird establishes Bird's Fort on the Trinity River, south of Birdville (present day Haltom City); Battle of Village Creek between Indians and forces led by General Edward H. Tarrant.

1843 General Edward H. Tarrant negotiates the Treaty of Bird's Fort, which opens the region to Anglo settlers.

1849 Major Ripley Arnold, U.S. Second Dragoons, founds Fort Worth on the banks of the Trinity River; the fort was later moved to the bluff top; Tarrant County is created from portions of Navarro County and the Peters Colony.

1856 First stage line brings U.S. Mail on July 18; Fort Worth chosen as county seat in a bitterly contested election.

1867 Mansfield Male and Female College, one of the earliest coeducational colleges in Texas, opens in Mansfield.

1870 Mosier Valley becomes the first freedman community in Tarrant County.

1873 Dr. W. P. Burts is elected first mayor of Fort Worth; city corporate charter issued; Indian raid near Azle is the last in the county.

1874 First telegraph line, from Fort Worth to Dallas, is installed.

1875 H. H. Butler opens private school for African-American children.

1876 Texas & Pacific Railway first arrives in Fort Worth from Dallas on July 19; mule-drawn streetcars operate between the courthouse square and the depot; first Fort Worth telephone links the home of Dr. W. B. Brooks and the drugstore; Bedford Post Office established in the home of W. W. Bobo.

1877 First artificial gas manufactured for lighting in Fort Worth.

1881 Texas & Pacific Railway builds line north of Fort Worth and renames the Athol community Keller in honor of John C. Keller, foreman of the railroad construction crew; Deer Creek is renamed Crowley for S. H. Crowley, an employee of the Gulf, Colorado and Santa Fe Railroad, when the rail line is built through the community.

1882 First public school opens in Fort Worth; Saginaw named for a local landowner's Michigan hometown.

1883 O'Bar community is renamed Azle following a quarrel between pioneer settlers William O'Bar and Dr. James Azle Steward.

1884 First home delivery of mail in Fort Worth.

1885 First electric lights in Fort Worth.

1888 St. Louis, Arkansas and Texas Railway, later called the St. Louis and Southwestern Railway or the Cotton Belt Route, arrives in Grapevine.

1889 Fort Worth Spring Palace, a community exhibition hall built of grain and other Texas products, opens in May; the palace burned in a spectacular fire at the end of the second season in 1890.

1890 Town of Mansfield incorporates.

1895 Present Tarrant County Courthouse completed in Fort Worth near the site of the original bluff-top fort.

1896 First Fat Stock Show is held under trees by Marine Creek on the North Side.

1901 Fort Worth Public Library opens.

1902 Armour and Swift meatpacking plants established; Interurban rail service between Fort Worth and Dallas inaugurated on July 1.

1903 First car on Fort Worth city streets; Chicago, Rock Island & Gulf Railway builds across William Letchworth Hurst's farm and names the nearby stop for him.

1904 Everman is named for an engineer on the International & Great Northern Railroad line.

1905 Theodore Roosevelt visits Fort Worth, the first president to do so.

1909 North Fort Worth annexed by Fort Worth; *Fort Worth Star* and *Fort Worth Telegram* combine to form the *Fort Worth Star-Telegram*.

1910 Southwestern Baptist Theological Seminary relocates to Fort Worth from Waco.

1911 Texas Christian University relocates to Fort Worth from Waco.

1914 Lake Worth formed by damming the West Fork of the Trinity River.

1917 Oil boom begins; Camp Bowie opens to train troops for World War I; U.S. aviators begin training at three airfields taken over from Canada.

1918 Famous aviator and ballroom dancer Vernon Castle is killed in an airplane crash at Carruthers Field in Benbrook.

1919 Saloons close because of prohibition.

1921 Radio station WBAP begins broadcasting; Fort Worth annexes Arlington Heights, Polytechnic Heights, and Riverside.

1922 Fort Worth annexes Niles City, the area containing the Fort Worth Stockyards.

1925 First airmail arrives; Fort Worth adopts city manager form of government; Fort Worth Historical Society founded (now Tarrant County Historical Society, Inc.)

1927 Fort Worth builds Meacham Field municipal airport.

1930 Lake Worth freezes over on January 18, attracting drivers and their cars onto the ice.

1934 Interurban service between Fort Worth and Dallas ceases.

1936 Frontier Centennial Exposition and Casa Mañana theater open in Fort Worth, celebrating the Texas Centennial.

1938 Texas Christian University fields a national champion football team.

1940 The *Como Weekly* begins publishing for the region's African-American community.

1941 Consolidated Vultee Aircraft builds bomber plant (now Lockheed Martin).

1942 U.S. Army builds Tarrant Field Aerodrome, precursor to Carswell Air Force Base (now Naval Air Station/Joint Reserve Base [NAS/JRB] Fort Worth Carswell Field).

1945 First Colonial National Invitational golf tournament played.

1947 WBAP is first television station in Texas.

1949 Haltom City incorporates, including the pioneer Birdville community.

1952 Lake Grapevine completed.

1953 Euless, named for pioneer businessman and Sheriff Elisha Adam Euless, incorporates.

1954 Fort Worth Art Museum opens, an outgrowth of art center originally housed in the library.

1956 Colleyville, named for pioneer physician Lilburn Howard Colley, incorporates.

1957 Dallas-Fort Worth Turnpike opens; it is the first toll road built in Texas.

1958 New Casa Mañana opens in Fort Worth.

1961 Amon Carter Museum opens in Fort Worth.

1962 Fort Worth hosts the first Van Cliburn International Piano Competition.

1963 Fort Worth public schools integrate first grade in compliance with court order; President John F. Kennedy speaks outside the Hotel Texas hours before he is assassinated in Dallas.

1967 Dr. Edward Guinn is elected as Fort Worth's first African-American city council member.

1971 Swift & Co. closes, ending packinghouse era.

1972 Kimbell Art Museum opens in Fort Worth.

1973 Dallas-Fort Worth Airport opens on January 13; American Airlines Flight 341 is the first to land.

1975 Fort Worth Water Garden completed; Fort Worth City Council single-member district plan adopted.

1977 Lenora Rolla founds the Tarrant County Black Historical and Genealogical Society.

1981 Sundance Square redevelopment project in downtown Fort Worth opens.

1986 Fort Worth celebrates the Texas Sesquicentennial.

1991 Western Currency Facility, operated by the Bureau of Printing and Engraving, opens.

1994 Carswell Air Force Base is transferred to the Department of the Navy and renamed Naval Air Station/Joint Reserve Base Fort Worth Carswell Field.

1999 Nancy Lee and Perry R. Bass Performance Hall opens in Fort Worth.

2000 Trinity Railway Express begins running between Fort Worth and Dallas.

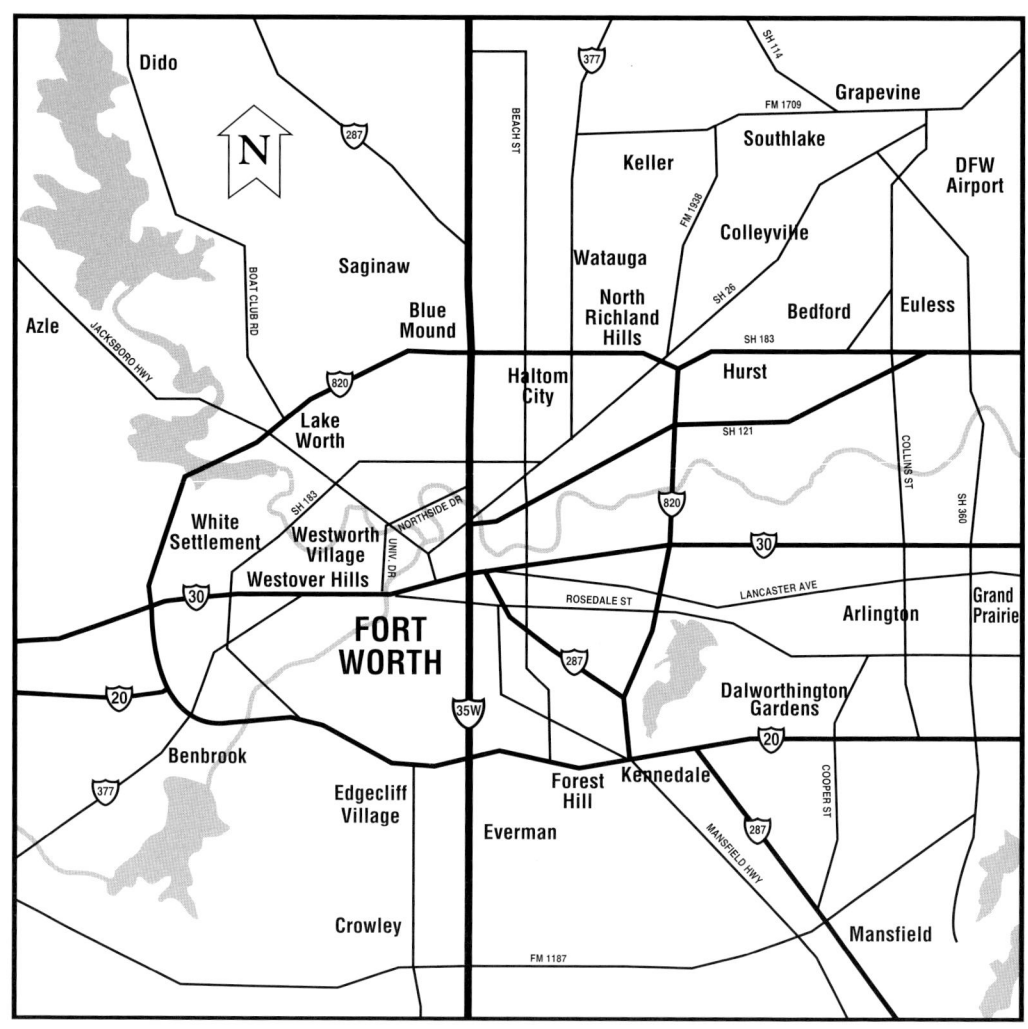

Tarrant County

How To Use This Book

This guide lists historic buildings and sites which have some type of official historical designation: listing on the National Register of Historic Places, Official Texas Historical Marker, or State Archeological Landmark. The information in this guide, however, is not limited to that found on historical markers.

Most of the buildings and sites are arranged geographically (see the map of Tarrant County which shows town locations) beginning with Fort Worth, the largest city, which is subdivided into five sections: Downtown, North Side, South Side, West Side, and Northeast/East Side. Next, cities in the county are listed alphabetically within three general geographic areas: Southeast, Northeast, and West Tarrant County. Cemeteries are listed alphabetically by the name of the cemetery in a category by themselves. A separate cemetery map shows the location of the listings in this category.

To locate the sites in a particular town or area, consult either the Table of Contents or the Index. The thematic tours group buildings and sites listed in the first section of the book by subject or interest area. The listings in this section are not complete, but rather refer to the main entries and maps in the geographic listings. Use the index (pages 169-180) to locate references to a specific building, site, person, neighborhood, town, or topic.

Area Maps

Fort Worth – Downtown   22
Fort Worth – North Side   46
Fort Worth – South Side   62
Fort Worth – West Side   78
Fort Worth – Northeast and East Side   90
Southeast Tarrant County
    Arlington   104
    Mansfield   112
Northeast Tarrant County
    Grapevine   118
West Tarrant County   130
Cemeteries   136

Definition of Terms

NR = Listed on the National Register of Historic Places

RTHL = Recorded Texas Historic Landmark (historic building, designated for architecture)

OTHM = Official Texas Historical Marker (subject marker)

SAL = State Archeological Landmark

Fort Worth–Downtown

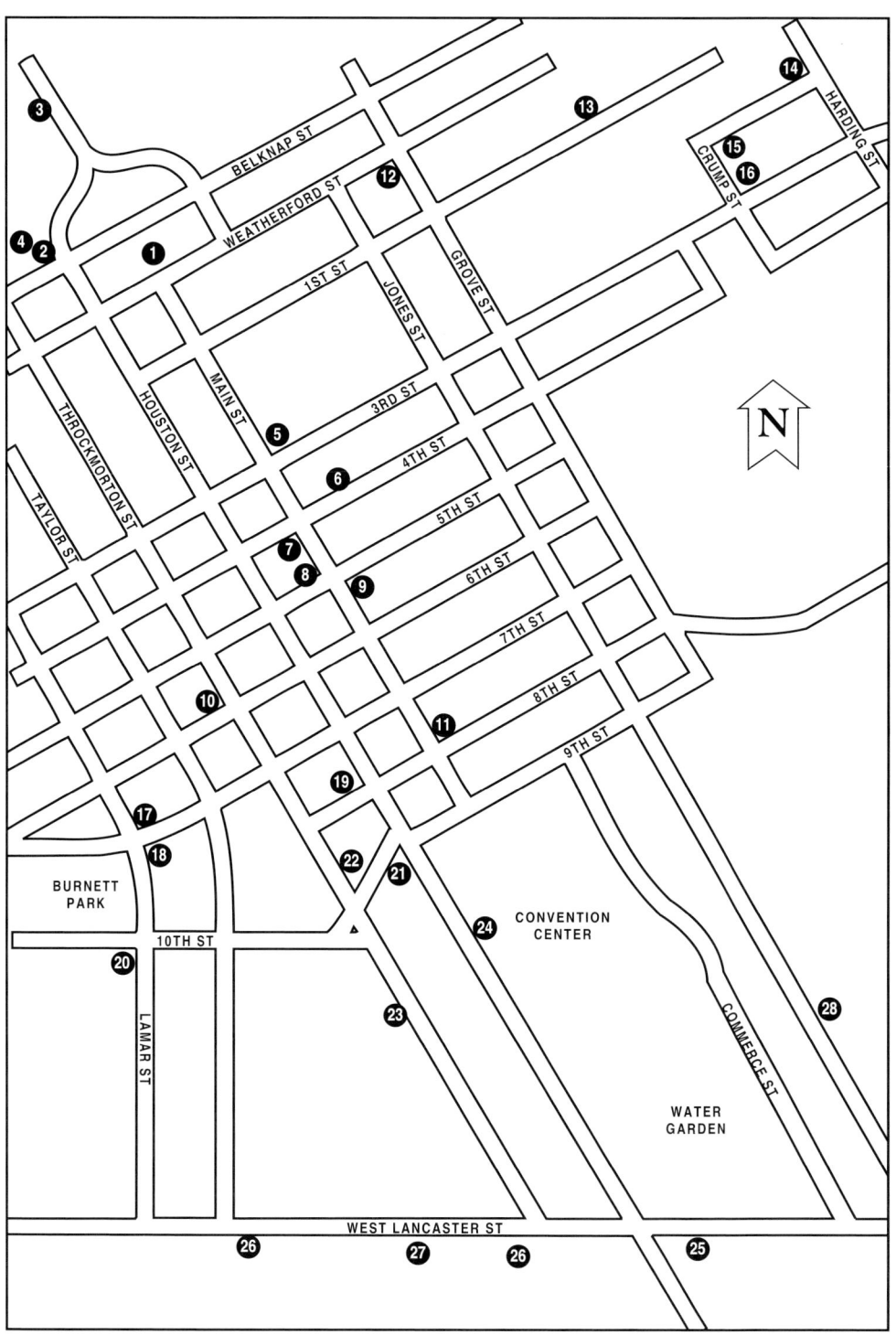

Fort Worth–Downtown

Downtown Fort Worth has Tarrant County's largest concentration of historic structures. Although nothing remains from the pre-railroad days – when most construction was small one and two-story wooden buildings – there are wonderful examples from the 1880s forward that showcase a wide variety of architectural styles. The buildings also tell the story of the forces that shaped Fort Worth's early growth – cattle, railroads, and oil. Within this section, the buildings and sites are grouped geographically so that it is easy to walk from one to another. It may be easier to drive to some parts of downtown – the early African-American neighborhood to the northeast, for example – but the separation also shows the very real geographic and social distance between white and African-American areas.

Downtown Fort Worth

1. Tarrant County Courthouse
2. Where the West Begins marker
3. Paddock Viaduct
4. Tarrant County Criminal Courts Building
5. Knights of Pythias Castle Hall
6. Land Title Block
7. Burk Burnett Building
8. Sinclair Building
9. Blackstone Hotel/Courtyard by Marriott
10. First Christian Church
11. Hotel Texas/Radisson Plaza
12. Texas State Teachers Association Building
13. Allen Chapel A.M.E. Church
14. Greater Saint James Baptist Church
15. Grand United Order of Odd Fellows Lodge No. 2144
16. Morning Chapel C.M.E. Church
17. Electric Building
18. Neil P. Anderson Building
19. W. T. Waggoner Building
20. United States Courthouse
21. Flatiron Building
22. Bryce Building
23. Saint Patrick Cathedral complex
24. Hell's Half Acre
25. Texas Spring Palace
26. Texas & Pacific Railway Terminal and Inbound Freight Warehouse
27. Fort Worth Main Post Office
28. Santa Fe Depot

Courthouse and Sundance Square

1. *Tarrant County Courthouse, 100 W. Weatherford, 1893-1895 (NR, RTHL & SAL)*

Set on the bluff overlooking the Trinity River, near where the old army post was established, the Tarrant County Courthouse is emblematic of both Tarrant County's history and its role as the seat of county government. The building was completed in 1895 at a cost of $408,380 – less than the budgeted allocation. The economy was depressed, however, and frustrated citizens turned all of the county commissioners out of office at the next election. Designed by the Kansas City firm of Gunn and Curtiss, this four-story red Texas granite building is a striking example of American Beaux Arts eclecticism, a classical style drawing inspiration from buildings of the French and Italian Renaissance. The building is designed to be impressive and signify the importance of the activities taking place inside. It is characterized by large structures with paired columns, balustrades, and pedimented entrances. As county government grew, the large courtroom spaces were subdivided and, in 1958, a Civil Courts Building was erected on the west side of the courthouse. In 1980 the decision was made to move county offices to a new facility and restore the courthouse as a house of courts, a project completed in 1983.

2. Fort Worth "Where the West Begins," 200 W. Belknap, (OTHM)

Fort Worth was founded on June 6, 1849, as a frontier post of Company F., 2nd Dragoons, 8th Department, United States Army, to guard the line between Anglo settlement to the east and Indian lands to the west. Thus, Fort Worth is often referred to as the place "Where the West Begins." Commander Major Ripley Arnold named the camp for his former superior officer, Major General William Jenkins Worth. In four years of operations, the post had but one serious Indian encounter. A town grew up alongside the fort, as a center for supply stores and stagecoach routes. In 1856, Fort Worth became the county seat of Tarrant County. A boom started after 1867 when millions of Longhorns were driven through town en route to Red River Crossing and Chisholm Trail. Herds forded the Trinity below Courthouse Bluff, one block north of this site. Cowboys got supplies for the long uptrail drive and caroused in taverns and dance halls. After the railroad arrived in 1876, increased cattle traffic won city the nickname of "Cowtown." City population tripled between 1900 and 1910, spurred by the arrival of the Armour and Swift meatpacking plants in 1902. Growth continued, based on varied multimillion-dollar industries of meatpacking, flour milling, grain storage, oil, aircraft plants, and military bases. Fort Worth also has developed as a center of culture, with universities, museums, art galleries, theaters, and a botanic garden. This historical marker is located near the site of the original fort.

3.Paddock Viaduct, Main Street, crossing Trinity River, 1913-1914 (NR, OTHM, & Texas Historic Civil Engineering Landmark)

A low-water crossing and ferries originally provided the only access across the Trinity River at this location, connecting the downtown area of Fort Worth with northern sections of the city. A two-lane suspension bridge, constructed near this site in the 1890s, proved inadequate for the growing population. This 1752-foot span, designed by the St. Louis firm of Brenneke and Fay, was the first concrete arch bridge in the United States to use self-supporting reinforcing steel. The bridge is named in honor of B. B. Paddock, a former Fort Worth newspaper editor, mayor, and state legislator. The bridge railings, sidewalks, and lighting date to 1965.

4. Tarrant County Criminal Courts Building, 200 W. Belknap Street, 1917-1918 (RTHL)

Built in 1917-1918, this structure is located on land upon which old Fort Worth was constructed in 1849. The noted Fort Worth architectural firm of Sanguinet and Staats designed the building, incorporating elements of the Beaux Arts and Classical Revival styles. In addition to a criminal courtroom, it originally housed the jail and gallows, a jail hospital, mental wards, and offices for the sheriff, district attorney, and district clerk.

5. Knights of Pythias Castle Hall, 315 Main Street, 1901 (NR & RTHL)

The Knights of Pythias, a charitable, benevolent, and fraternal order, built their first castle hall on this site in 1881, but it was destroyed by fire in 1901. Local architect Marshall Sanguinet made slight revisions to the earlier design, and the hall was rebuilt in a style that resembles a Dutch or Flemish medieval guildhall. The Pythians leased space on the first and sec-

ond floors, which provided funds to maintain the building, and reserved the third floor for their own meeting rooms. The group sold the building in 1975. The knight, who occupies a niche at the top of the front façade and is probably the most distinctive part of this unique building, is a replica crafted in 1983 after the original knight from the 1881 building was severely damaged in a fall. Long a local favorite, the Knights of Pythias Castle Hall was one of the first buildings in Fort Worth to be designated as a Recorded Texas Historic Landmark, an honor it received in 1962.

6. Land Title Block, 111 E. Fourth Street, 1889 (RTHL)

Built to house a mortgage bank, real estate development company, and law office, the Land Title Block is Fort Worth's best surviving nineteenth-century commercial building. True to the Victorian ideal of richly ornamented design, it features a wide variety of materials including carved sandstone, multi-colored glazed brick, decorative patterned brick, stained glass, and cast iron. This two-story building was typical of Fort Worth's commercial streetscape when it was built, but today the small building stands alone on a city block filled by a parking lot and surrounded by buildings that tower over it. Pioneer architects Haggart and Sanguinet designed the building, and it remains one of Marshall Sanguinet's earliest surviving buildings. The sandstone carving on the east façade of the building features an owl, tree, and mockingbird along with the initials of the Ross, Head and Ross law firm, which occupied offices on the second floor of the building.

7. Burk Burnett Building, 500-502 Main Street, 1914 (NR)

The State National Bank, with E. Baldridge as president, secured the architectural firm of Sanguinet and Staats to design its headquarters. With Buchanan and Gilder as contractors, the building was completed in 1914. By 1915, the bank had failed and one of Texas' leading citizens, Samuel Burk Burnett, bought the property and affixed his name to the front. Burnett, a former trail driver, was the owner of the famed 6666 Ranch, a founder of the Texas and Southwestern Cattle Raisers Association, and the first president of the Southwestern Exposition and Fat Stock Show. Towering twelve stories into the sky, it was the tallest and most modern building in town when it was built. Four huge Corinthian columns of polished granite two stories high form the base of the building, topped by a relatively plain eight-story shaft. The most delightful portion of the building is the top two stories, which have fanciful white terra cotta ornamentation.

8. Sinclair Building, 512 Main Street, 1929-1930 (NR & RTHL)

Pioneer oilman Richard O. Dulaney hired noted Fort Worth architect Wiley G. Clarkson to design this building. The owners made a concerted effort to design the most up-to-date skyscraper in the city. To that end, they and the architect visited Chicago, Detroit, and New York City before

finalizing the design. The building acquired its name from the Sinclair Oil Company which leased offices here soon after the building's completion.

Built during the city's oil- and gas-inspired golden era, the sixteen-story Zigzag Moderne building features Mayan-inspired detailing in the Monel (a trade name for alloy of nickel and copper) screen above the main entrance, in the stepped-fret design (a geometric pattern of repeated horizontal and vertical lines) in the limestone parapets, and in the corbeled (projecting) arch surrounds flanking the ground-floor elevator openings. The attention to detail, the rich surface treatments, and sophisticated building design make the Sinclair Building one of Fort Worth's finest examples of the Art Deco (Zigzag Moderne) style.

9. Blackstone Hotel/Courtyard by Marriott Downtown-Blackstone, 601 Main Street, 1929 (NR & RTHL)

The first Art Deco-style skyscraper in Fort Worth, the Blackstone Hotel was erected in 1929 for wealthy cattleman C. A. "Gus" O'Keefe, who named it after a visit to the Blackstone Hotel in Chicago. The city's first radio station, WBAP, once occupied the twenty-second (top) floor. A five-story annex, with a pool on its roof, was added in the 1950s by the Hilton Hotel chain, which occupied the building from 1952 to 1962. The hotel features setback upper levels with terraces, which provide outstanding views of the city. Slender brick piers, which divide the structure's facade into bays, are capped by ornate terra cotta finials. While not strictly Art Moderne or Art Deco in its design, the Blackstone reflects the popularity of these styles in its massing and details.

10. First Christian Church, 612 Throckmorton, 1914-1915 (NR & OTHM)

Founded in 1855 by the Reverend A. M. Dean, First Christian is the oldest church congregation in Fort Worth. By 1910, the membership had risen to over three thousand and had outgrown the church erected on this same site in 1878. In 1912, with the financial support of Major K. M. Van Zandt, a prominent banker, and cattleman Samuel Burk Burnett, architects E. W. Van Slyke and Clyde Woodruff were hired to design the new building. The First Christian Church in Fort Worth is an imposing Neoclassical structure designed in a Greek cross plan. Crowned by a copper dome, the church's exterior is dominated by a pair of Corinthian porticoes. The interior features include the Akron or auditorium-plan main sanctuary, with flooring raked toward the altar which is in the northwest corner, fine stained-glass dome and windows, and a theater area adjacent to the main sanctuary which can be linked with the sanctuary by raising a large partition wall.

11. Hotel Texas /Radisson Plaza Fort Worth, 815 Main Street, 1921 (NR & RTHL)

In 1919 the Citizens Hotel Company, a group composed of outstanding city leaders, engaged the local architectural firm of Sanguinet and Staats to design a hotel which they hoped would become the finest in the South. Their efforts resulted in construction of the Hotel Texas, which was completed in 1921. Rising fifteen stories above the city, the hotel is an aesthetically pleasing blend of architectural styles, most strongly inspired by the formal Georgian Revival style. A Fort Worth touch is found in the architrave which features cow skulls draped with chains of flowers from the yucca plant. President John F. Kennedy stayed here on the eve of his assassination in 1963. The hotel was extensively remodeled in 1979, and it has operated since 1991 as the Radisson Plaza.

12. Texas State Teachers Association Building, 410 E. Weatherford, 1930 (RTHL)

Completed in 1930, this building was constructed to serve as the headquarters of the Texas State Teachers Association. Noted Fort Worth architect Wiley G. Clarkson designed the Renaissance Revival structure. In 1949 the TSTA moved its offices to Austin, and the Texas and Southwestern Cattle Raisers Association, which officed here for thirty years, later purchased the building.

Near Northeast

Several historic church buildings still stand in what was once a thriving African-American neighborhood northeast of downtown Fort Worth. It was one of Fort Worth's oldest African-American residential areas and, during segregation, housed businesses, clubs, and churches that served the community. Almost all of the historic folk or vernacular wood-frame houses have been replaced by contemporary duplex and triplex rental residences built in 1997 as the Hillside Apartments. One charming home that remains is the circa 1898 cottage with angled bays located at 908 E. Third Street.

13. Allen Chapel African Methodist Episcopal Church, 116 Elm Street, 1912-1914 (NR & RTHL)

Since its dedication on July 22, 1914, the Allen Chapel African Methodist Episcopal Church, an imposing two-story Tudor Gothic Revival sanctuary, has housed one of Fort Worth's oldest African-American congregations. Designed by nationally known African-American architect William Sidney Pittman, son-in-law of educator Booker T. Washington, this handsome, yellow-brick, rectangular edifice with bell tower is one of the more architecturally sophisticated early-twentieth-century black churches in the Southwest. The two-story structure sits on a raised basement and features excellent art-glass windows, two entrances that flank the main altar, a historical Estey pipe organ, and a handsome suspended, horseshoe-shaped balcony. Pittman (1875-1958), who trained at Tuskegee Institute and Drexel Institute in Philadelphia, moved to Dallas in 1912. Allen Chapel is one of only a few surviving Texas buildings designed by Pittman during his sixteen-year Texas career.

14. Greater Saint James Baptist Church, 210 Harding Street, 1913-1918 (NR & RTHL)

The Reverend J. Francis Robinson and members of Fort Worth's first African-American Baptist congregation, Mount Gilead Baptist Church,

founded Saint James Baptist Church in 1895. The worshipers first met in another organization's building while they raised funds for their own church home. Construction of this structure began in 1913, and services were held in the basement until the sanctuary was completed in 1918. Frank J. Singleton was the architect, and African-American contractor George Powell built the south wing, while B. G. Rhodes built the north wing. Short square entry towers frame the Gothic Revival style red-brick building, and, along with the lancet-shaped art glass windows, give it a fortress-like appearance.

15. Grand United Order of Odd Fellows, Lodge No. 2144, 612 Grove, 1926 (OTHM)

Organized in 1880, the Odd Fellows were an active force in Fort Worth's African-American community during the early years of the twentieth century. Associated with a national order that had been charted in 1843, the local lodge supported various charities and conducted seminars and professional business training sessions. Lodge members built this structure in 1926 and held their meetings on the second floor until they disbanded in 1937. It stands as one of the few reminders of the original black business district in Fort Worth.

16. Morning Chapel C.M.E. Church, 903 E. Third Street, 1934-1936, 1958 (NR)

Morning Chapel was established as Morning Chapel Colored Methodist Episcopal Church in 1868. This building, designed by local architect W. C. Meador, was built in 1934-1936. Cornerstones from two previous buildings that housed this historic congregation are set next to the cornerstone for the current structure. Constructed of rusticated limestone blocks, with stone buttresses at each corner of the building and a series of arched windows that give the structure a Gothic Revival impression, Morning Chapel anchors the block on which it stands. Although new multi-family units have replaced the small single-family residences that once surrounded the church, it remains a vibrant community institution. The name of the church was changed to Morning Chapel Christian Methodist Episcopal in 1954, and in 1958 a brick education building was erected to the rear of the main church by African-American contractor Joe Peace.

Mid-town

17. Electric Building, 410 W. 7th Street, 1927-1929 (NR)

The Electric Building occupies a commanding location in Fort Worth's urban landscape, diagonally across from one of the downtown's primary open spaces, Burnett Park. The Fort Worth Power and Light Company originally occupied the basement and first six floors of the building, with the other floors leased as offices. Constructed between 1927 and 1929 under the supervision of architect Wyatt C. Hedrick, the building features detailing influenced by the Art Deco and Spanish Renaissance Revival styles. Some of the details relate directly to its use by an electric company – hands that grasp lightning bolts alternate with cut-stone diamonds in a series of cartouches ringing the building. A six-story annex on the north side of the eighteen-story tower, completed in 1929-1930, housed the Hollywood Theatre. The Electric Building was renovated in 1996 to provide 106 apartment units, and the theater was converted into a parking garage.

18. Neil P. Anderson Building, 411 W. Seventh Street, 1921 (NR & RTHL)

Designed by the architectural firm of Sanguinet and Staats, the Neil P. Anderson Building's main tenant was the Neil P. Anderson Cotton Company. Anderson died before the building was built, but his son, Bernie Anderson, and son-in-law, Morris Berney, continued to run the firm and had this structure erected. Other grain and cotton companies were also housed here, as were the Fort Worth Cotton and Grain Exchange and United States Department of Agriculture offices. Distinguished by a graceful curving façade that fronts onto Burnett Park and West Seventh Street, the eleven-story brick structure has windows that curve to follow the lines of the building and decorative terra cotta medallions depicting bales of cotton and stems of grain. The Neil P. Anderson Cotton Company's skylit cotton showroom occupied the eleventh floor for many years. Here cotton was separated and graded, a process that required good, even lighting. Slated for demolition by the late 1970s, this building was rescued and rehabilitated for general office use in 1977, making it an early central business district revitalization effort.

19. W. T. Waggoner Building, 810 Houston Street, 1920 (NR)

Since its completion in 1920, the W. T. Waggoner Building has stood as a physical manifestation of the crucial role played by Fort Worth in the

national oil boom. W. T. Waggoner was one of a handful of cattlemen who became multi-millionaires due to oil discoveries on their ranches. In 1919, Waggoner invested part of his fortune in a new office building, both to diversify his financial investments and as a monument to his wealth and power. The building, originally planned for sixteen stories, was ultimately constructed with twenty, for a total height of 210 feet, making it the tallest in the Southwest at the time. It is a Texas version of the Chicago School skyscraper style, designed by the prominent Fort Worth firm of Sanguinet and Staats. The building was intended to be the ultimate in modern offices, featuring the latest conveniences such as elevators, refrigerated drinking water from an artesian well on the property, Austral windows – steel windows that looked like ordinary double-hung windows but which tilted to provide seventy per-cent ventilation instead of the typical fifty per-cent when the window was open – and a built-in vacuum cleaning system. Begun in March 1919, the building was completed one year later at a final cost of $1,500,000.

20. United States Courthouse, 501 W. Tenth Street, 1933-1934 (NR)

Renowned Philadelphia architect Paul Philippe Cret and Fort Worth-based Wiley G. Clarkson, who served as associate architect, designed this

handsome Classic Moderne building to house federal district and appeals courts. It faces Burnett Park, long a gathering place for downtown workers. The United States Courthouse was a Depression-era project, completed in 1934, and its design combines the formal balance of classical architecture with contemporary Moderne detailing, including polished aluminum window panels and grillwork with geometric, Pueblo Indian, Plains Indian arrow, and Egyptian lotus motifs. The United States Appeals Courtroom on the fourth floor houses the only examples of Depression-era public art in Fort Worth. Two murals, "The Taking of Sam Bass," and "Texas Rangers in Camp," were painted by Frank A. Mechau, Jr., as part of the United States Treasury Department's Section of Fine Arts program and installed in 1940.

21. Flatiron Building, 1000 Houston Street, 1907 (NR & RTHL)

Fort Worth's earliest surviving skyscraper, the Flatiron Building, was designed by Sanguinet and Staats and inspired by the original 1902 New York City Flatiron Building. The building is an important regional interpretation of the Chicago School style in which architects designed buildings to emphasize their verticality and used steel-frame construction and elevators to make them practical. Dr. Bacon Saunders, a surgeon, erected this building to house his medical offices and leased space to other physicians. One significant

regional variation is the presence of a belt course featuring panther heads. Before the railroad arrived in Fort Worth in 1876, a Dallas newspaper charged that Fort Worth was such a sleepy little town that a panther could sleep undisturbed in its streets. Citizens, refusing to be insulted, began to call Fort Worth "Panther City." Today, one of two sleeping panther sculptures in downtown Fort Worth is located on the west side of the Flatiron Building.

22. Bryce Building, 909 Throckmorton, 1910 (NR & RTHL)

Leading Fort Worth businessman and civic leader William J. Bryce built this structure in 1910 to house the offices of his construction firm, the Bryce Building Company. Bryce erected many of the city's commercial buildings and served as mayor of Fort Worth from 1927 to 1933. The Bryce Building is a simply detailed, two-story masonry structure designed in the Renaissance Revival style. The curious form of the diminutive building follows the property line of the small, five-sided lot on which the building was constructed. Bryce maintained personal offices on the first floor and leased out the second floor to a number of local groups and organizations. Once hidden behind the old Fort Worth Public Library building, the Bryce Building became more visible when the 1938 library building was demolished for a parking lot in 1990.

23. Saint Patrick Cathedral Complex, 1206 Throckmorton, 1888-1892 (NR & RTHL)

Stately and imposing, the Gothic Revival Saint Patrick Cathedral is Fort Worth's oldest functioning church building. Built of locally quarried limestone according to plans drawn by James J. Kane, Fort Worth's first professional architect, the church has a basilica plan with a nave, apse, and side aisles. The east façade is flanked by two buttressed towers, originally designed to hold spires that were never built. The church interior, which features a handsome rose window above the main entrance, was extensively renovated in 1946-1947, giving it a more ornate Baroque air. Saint Patrick was built as a church, but was designated as Saint Patrick Cathedral in 1969 when it became the seat of the new Diocese of Fort Worth.

Saint Ignatius Academy. 1206 Throckmorton, 1888-1889

The first Catholic school in Fort Worth, Saint Ignatius Academy was organized by the Sisters of Saint Mary of Namur in 1885. This four-story limestone structure, used for classrooms and chapel, was completed in 1889. Opposite sides of the square building are roughly symmetrical. James J. Kane designed the building, which is the major surviving example of the Second Empire style in Fort Worth. School classes were conducted here until 1962, and the building is now used for Saint Patrick Cathedral functions.

Saint Patrick Church Rectory, 1206 Throckmorton, 1908

Built in 1908 adjacent to Saint Patrick Church on the site of the old Saint Stanislaus Church, the rectory provided living and workspace for priests. Originally built of red brick but now painted white, the Prairie-Style structure still serves as the cathedral rectory.

Water Garden Area

Historically, the southern end of Fort Worth's central business district was home to the city's thriving railroad industry and businesses that either supported or needed access to the railroad. Today, the wholesale businesses, restaurants, hotels, and saloons are gone, but several historic railroad buildings remain. Most of Hell's Half Acre, home to the city's red light district, was bulldozed during the mid-1960s to make way for the Fort Worth Convention Center, and the remainder replaced by the Fort Worth Water Garden, designed by the internationally known architects Philip Johnson and John Burgee. Completed in 1974, the Water Garden uses concrete, water, and dense vegetation to create a grouping of three dynamic water features around a central plaza.

24. Hell's Half Acre, 12th & Houston streets (OTHM)

A notorious red-light district known as Hell's Half Acre developed in this section of Fort Worth after the arrival of the Texas & Pacific Railway in 1876 launched a local economic boom. Fort Worth was soon the favorite destination for hundreds of cowboys, buffalo hunters, railroad workers, and freighters eager to wash off the trail dust and enjoy themselves. The saloons, dance halls, gambling houses, and bordellos in Hell's Half Acre were tolerated by city officials because of their importance to the town's economy. The district prospered in the 1880s and added to Fort Worth's growing reputation as a rowdy frontier town. Famous gamblers Luke Short, Bat Masterson, and Wyatt Earp and outlaws Sam Bass, Eugene Bunch, Butch Cassidy, and the Sundance Kid are known to have spent time in Hell's Half Acre. Repeated efforts to clean up the district proved unsuccessful until army officers at Camp Bowie, established here during World War I, helped local officials shut it down.

25. Texas Spring Palace/Al Hayne Monument, 100 block, W. Lancaster Avenue, 1893 (OTHM)

Following a suggestion by General R. A. Cameron, an officer of the Fort Worth & Denver Railway, city promoters developed the idea of an annual exhibition for the display of Texas agricultural products. In 1889 they constructed the Texas Spring Palace near this site to house the exhibits. Designed by the Fort Worth firm of

Armstrong and Messer, it was an exotic, two-story, domed wooden structure decorated with flowers, seeds, and grasses. On the evening of May 30, 1890, as some seven thousand people attended a dress ball, a fire swept through the Spring Palace, completely destroying the structure. A number of people inside had to leap from the second floor to escape the flames, and the Palace reportedly collapsed within eleven minutes. According to *Frank Leslie's Illustrated Newspaper*, Alfred S. Hayne, a British civil engineer, "picked up fainting women and terrified children, and dropped them out of the second story windows into willing arms." The only fatality of the fire, he died the next day of burns suffered in the rescue effort. In 1893, the Women's Humane Association dedicated a monument in memory of his heroism and courage.

26. *Texas & Pacific Railway Terminal and Inbound Freight Warehouse, 1600 Throckmorton (West Lancaster Avenue at Main Street) and 250 Block West Lancaster Avenue (West Lancaster Avenue at Jennings Avenue), 1930-1931 (NR, both buildings, & RTHL, terminal only)*

The Texas & Pacific Railway arrived in Fort Worth in 1876, providing a vital boost to the economic growth of the city. This complex is part of a public-private works project begun during the early years of the Great Depression and led by President John L. Lancaster of the T&P, for whom Lancaster Avenue is named. These stunning Moderne or Art Deco style buildings were built on the southern edge of the central business district in 1930-1931 to replace a Victorian-era terminal. Local architect and engineer Wyatt C. Hedrick designed both the thirteen-story terminal and the eight-story Inbound Freight Warehouse. The elegant terminal building is a solid rectangular mass with towers defining each corner. It is ornamented by cast-stone stylized geometric forms, plant motifs, and eagles. Inside, the waiting rooms and elevator lobby are decorated with a gold-leaf-encrusted plaster ceiling, ornate chandeliers, and marble floors, all restored to their original splendor in 1999. Architect Earl Koeppe designed most of these decorative elements. Off the main waiting room were two subsidiary waiting rooms, one for white women and the other for African Americans. A smaller elevator lobby on the west side of the building served the office tower, which housed railroad and government offices. Today the terminal serves the Trinity Railway Express commuter train, which offers service between Fort Worth and Dallas.

The Inbound Freight Warehouse is an elongated rectangular mass of yellow buff textured brick that complements the design of the more ornate terminal building. The now vacant building, which had an enormous refrigerated warehouse on its west end (note the lack of windows), served as a storage and transfer facility for goods shipped to the area by rail.

27. Fort Worth Main Post Office, 251 W. Lancaster Avenue, 1931-1933 (NR & RTHL)

The Fort Worth Post Office was established in 1856 with pioneer set-tler Julian Feild serving as postmaster. The central offices were moved to this building, at the corner of Jennings and Lancaster avenues, near the railroad line that handled much of the mail, in 1933. Designed by the Fort Worth firm of Wyatt C. Hedrick, the Beaux Arts/Classical Revival building features a Cordova limestone exterior and interior detailing of marble, bronze, and gold leaf. Exterior ornamentation reflects the sig-nificance of the cattle industry in Fort Worth. Note the Longhorn and Polled Hereford cattle on the column capitals. Construction began in 1931, and the jobs provided by this development, along with nearby rail-road projects, helped blunt the effect of the Depression in Fort Worth. When the Jack D. Watson Post Office opened in 1986 in North Fort Worth, this facility ceased to serve as the central mail processing facili-ty, but it continues to provide window and box service.

28. Santa Fe Depot, 1501 Jones Street, 1899; 1901 (RTHL)

Until Amtrak rail service moved to Fort Worth's Intermodal Transportation Center north of this building in 2002, the Santa Fe Depot had the distinction of being the only depot to offer more than a century of continuous rail service to Fort Worth. Built in 1899 when Fort Worth was a major hub of railroad traffic, the station was first called Fort Worth Union Depot because six rail lines operated out of the facility. It kept operating through a 1901 fire, a 1938 remodeling, and the demise of many of the rail lines that once served the city. Although the Beaux Arts style station is not large and is in only fair condition, it retains a wealth of detailing including alternating bands of limestone and red brick, diamond-patterned brickwork between the first and second stories, large arched windows, and a pressed metal, barrel-vaulted ceiling. At one time, the depot housed painted glass windows depicting the history of western travel from Pony Express to steam locomotives, but they are now preserved by the Pate Museum of Transportation, three miles north of Cresson.

Fort Worth–North Side

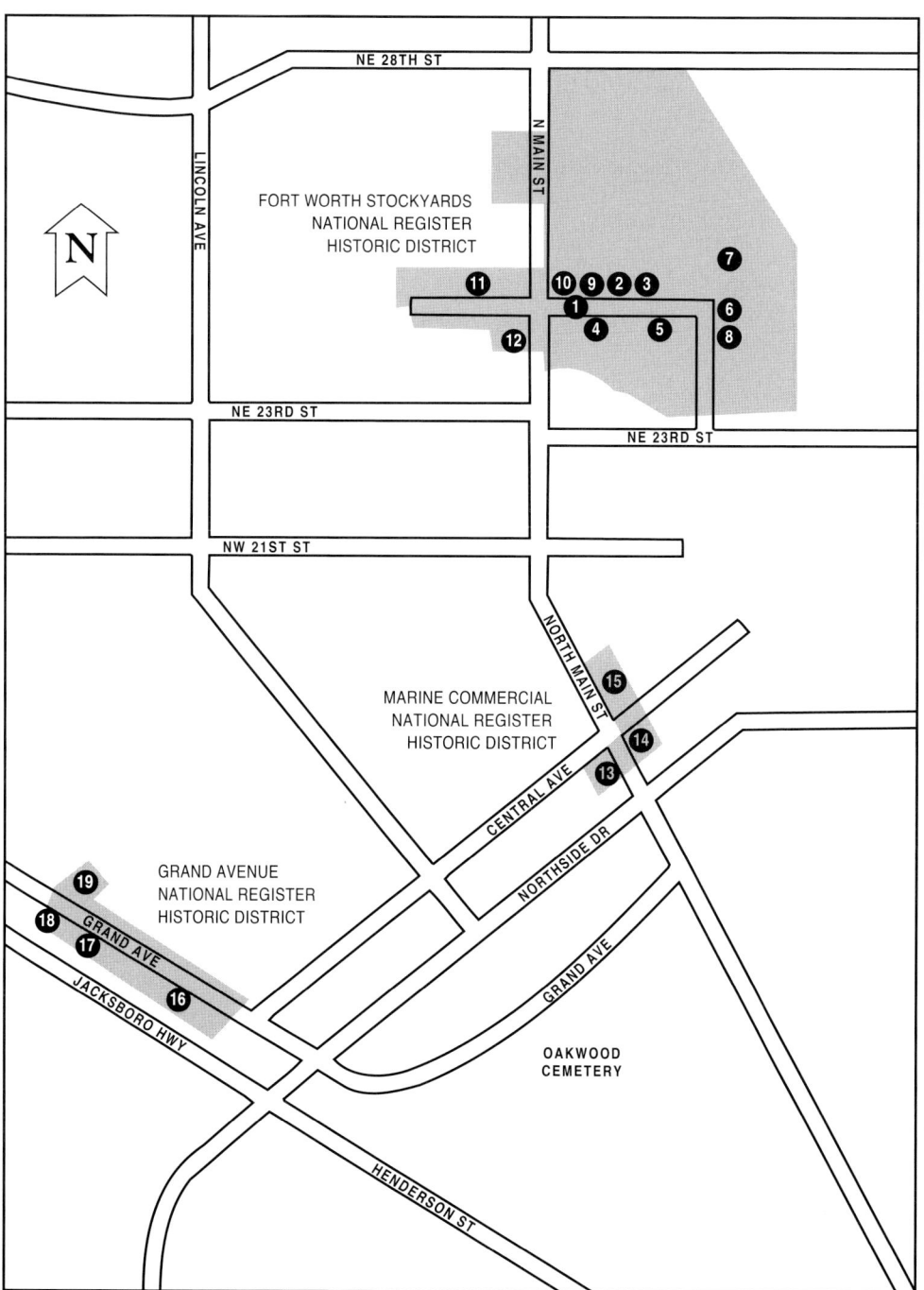

N

NE 28TH ST

LINCOLN AVE

N MAIN ST

FORT WORTH STOCKYARDS
NATIONAL REGISTER
HISTORIC DISTRICT

⑪ ⑩⑨❷❸ ❼
❶ ❻
⑫ ❹ ❺ ❽

NE 23RD ST

NE 23RD ST

NW 21ST ST

NORTH MAIN ST

MARINE COMMERCIAL
NATIONAL REGISTER
HISTORIC DISTRICT ⑮

CENTRAL AVE ⑭

⑬

NORTHSIDE DR

GRAND AVENUE ⑲
NATIONAL REGISTER
HISTORIC DISTRICT
⑱ GRAND AVE
⑰
⑯

GRAND AVE

JACKSBORO HWY

OAKWOOD
CEMETERY

HENDERSON ST

Fort Worth–North Side

Fort Worth Stockyards National Register Historic District

The Fort Worth Stockyards National Register Historic District is the heart of Fort Worth's "Cowtown." Cattle were first driven through Fort Worth after the Civil War, and several attempts were made in the late 1800s to establish slaughterhouses. It was not until the Armour and Swift facilities were opened in 1902, however, that Fort Worth became a major player in the sale of livestock and in the meatprocessing industry. This historic district includes the remains of the Armour and Swift plants, the buildings where animals were shown and sold, and the commercial structures that provided lodging and services for ranchers and stockyards employees. Although some livestock trading and rodeos still take place here, the stockyards area was largely reborn as an historic entertainment district after slaughterhouse operations ended in the early 1970s.

North Side

Fort Worth Stockyards National Register Historic District
1. Fort Worth Stock Yards Sign
2. Coliseum
3. Fort Worth Live Stock Exchange
4. Horse & Mule Barns
5. Hog & Sheep Pens
6. Exchange Avenue Stairs/Armour & Swift Plaza
7. Armour & Co. Packing and Provision Plant
8. Swift & Co. Meatpacking Plant and Office Building
9. Stock Yards National Bank
10. Thannisch Block/Stockyards Hotel
11. Eddlebrock Commercial Building
12. New Isis Theater

Marine Commercial National Register Historic District
13. Fort Worth Laundry Co.
14. Greines Furniture Co./Mulholland Co.
15. Rose/Roseland/Marine Theater

Grand Avenue National Register Historic District
16. Whalen-Jary House
17. House
18. Armstrong House
19. Waddy R. Ross House

1. Fort Worth Stock Yards Sign, 100 block, E. Exchange Avenue, 1910

This sign officially marked the western boundary of the Stock Yards Company property. To the east were acres of pens and buildings that housed livestock exhibition and sale operations. To the west were commercial businesses that fed, clothed, housed, and entertained those who came to conduct business in the stockyards. The sign sits atop a bridge built to span Marine Creek, visible by taking the walkway between buildings to the south that leads to a path along the creek.

2. Coliseum, 123 E. Exchange Avenue, 1907-1908 (SAL & OTHM)

Until 1908, the predecessor of the annual Fort Worth Fat Stock Show was held in a variety of outdoor locations near the stockyards. As interest increased in the event and its educational and promotional values were realized, livestock exhibitors sought a permanent home for the show. The Coliseum was constructed in 1907-1908 to provide such an exhibition hall, and the stock show was held here annually for thirty-four years. Both the Stock Yards Company and the Armour and Swift meatpacking plants financed the construction of the Coliseum because they recognized its value in promoting the livestock industry. The world's first indoor rodeo was held here in 1918, and the Coliseum has been the site of numerous other community events including a revival preached by evangelist Billy Sunday, an appearance by President Theodore Roosevelt, and performances by Enrico Caruso, Elvis Presley, and Harry James. Designed in the Mission Revival style to complement the Live Stock Exchange, the Coliseum has fourteen thousand square feet of unobscured interior space thanks to a system of hinged steel trusses.

3. *Fort Worth Live Stock Exchange, 131 E. Exchange Avenue, 1902-1903 (RTHL)*

The Live Stock Exchange building is at the center of the Fort Worth Stock Yards National Register Historic District. It was also the nerve center of stockyards operations, housing the Stock Yards Company and many livestock commission company offices. Here, transactions concerning the sale of livestock held in the acres of pens that once surrounded the building were processed before the animals made their way to the packing plants up the hill or back to the ranch. The graceful Mission Revival style building, with its Alamo-style parapet and Longhorn sculpture, is one of Fort Worth's best-known buildings. The Longhorn, affectionately called "Molly," is the symbol of the historic stockyards district. The building still houses some offices for livestock-related enterprises, but the most popular tenant is the North Fort Worth Historic Society's museum on the first floor, which tells the story of the stockyards and North Fort Worth.

4. Horse & Mule Barns, 122-124 E. Exchange Avenue, 1911-1912 (OTHM)

With many wooden buildings, fire was a constant threat in the stockyards. After the original horse and mule barns burned in 1911, the Stock Yards Company decided to rebuild them in brick and stucco. The Mission Revival parapet above each barn entry echoes the style of the nearby Live Stock Exchange building. During the First World War – when draft animals were needed for the cavalry and to pull military equipment – Fort Worth was the largest horse-and-mule market in the world. Demand decreased as motorized vehicles replaced animals for farming and military purposes, but the area between the two rows of barns is still known today as "Mule Alley."

5. Hog & Sheep Pens/Stockyards Station, 200 block E. Exchange Avenue, 1911 (OTHM)

As the number of animals sold through the Live Stock Exchange increased, more facilities were needed to hold them. In 1903, 150,527 hogs were processed through the Armour and Swift packing plants, but by 1917 that number had increased to 1,062,021. These covered fire-proof pens were built in 1911 to house sheep and hogs. Underground tunnels and ramps led to the packing houses up the hill, and the facility was serviced by an extensive underground sewer system. The pens sat vacant for decades after the packing plants closed, but in 1992 they were redeveloped to house a shopping and entertainment complex. The concrete posts and brick floors are original, and the generally open nature of the facility has been preserved, but most of the pens have been replaced by storefronts.

6. Exchange Avenue Stairs/Armour & Swift Plaza, 1902; 1912
   Every workday, streetcars unloaded at the foot of these stairs, and workers climbed the stairs to reach their jobs at the meatpacking plants. The Armour and Swift company names flanking the stairs identified the industrial complex and provided an impressive gateway for workers and visitors alike.

7. Armour & Co. Packing and Provision Plant, 400-700 blocks E. Exchange Avenue (north side), 1902-1958
   The entire east end of the Fort Worth Stockyards National Register Historic District contains the original the Armour and Swift packing plants. Located on a small hill overlooking the rest of the district, the two packing plants once dominated the industrial complex. In 1932, the Armour plant had a daily processing capacity of 1200 cattle, 1400 calves, 2800 sheep, and 1850 hogs. Although a number of buildings have been demolished since the plant ceased meatpacking operations in 1962 –

some for bricks to build other structures in the area – many original buildings still remain. The cluster of buildings closest to Exchange Avenue still contains a fat refinery and oil processing plant, as it did when the meatpacking plant was open.

8. Swift & Co. Meatpacking Plant and Swift & Co. General Office Building, 600-700 blocks E. Exchange Avenue (south side), 1902-1955

From Exchange Avenue, the most visible structure in the Swift & Co. complex is the old General Office Building, with its two-story porch wrapping around three sides of the building. Behind it, to the east, are the hulking remains of the meatpacking plant, including the partially demolished killing tank with its distinctive mushroom-shaped columns. Cattle walked up an outside ramp to the top floor of the building and were "disassembled" on the way down. Other buildings contained a lard-making facility and a fertilizer house, with buttresses that reinforced the building in case of an explosion. The old Swift property is bounded on three sides by a brick wall. An entrance gate at the southern border of the property has an attractive curved double stairway with the Swift logo leading to a double set of iron gates.

9. Stock Yards National Bank/Fincher's, 115-119 E. Exchange Avenue, 1910

Although this structure is the westernmost building constructed by the Fort Worth Stock Yards Company, it traditionally housed businesses that supported the stockyards rather than direct livestock industry operations.

Built atop the Marine Creek Bridge, this Mission Revival style building housed the Stock Yards National Bank until 1933. Through the years, it has also been home to a number of clothing stores and dry goods stores. The companion building across the street was built at the same time and has housed a number of restaurants and saloons.

10. Thannisch Block/Stockyards Hotel, 101-109 E. Exchange Avenue, 1906-1907; 1913 (RTHL)

Colonel Thomas M. Thannisch was an entrepreneur who made the most of the need for services of those coming to do business in the stockyards. After opening a saloon nearby in 1902, he bought this prime corner location at the intersection of Main and Exchange avenues in 1904 and opened the Stock Yards Club Saloon which had a bar on the ground floor and furnished rooms for rent upstairs. Thannisch built the first part of this hotel in 1906-1907 and expanded it in 1913, although the two sections of the building are well integrated. Again, the first floor held retail businesses, while hotel rooms on the second and third floors were rented to ranchers and salesmen doing business in the stockyards. After the packing plants closed, the hotel fell on hard times. As the area changed from a livestock market to an historical and entertainment area, there was again a need for a hotel. The Thannisch Block was renovated in 1984 and today operates as the fifty-two-room Stockyards Hotel.

11. Edlebrock Commercial Building/Stock Yards Lodge No. 1244, 124 W. Exchange Avenue, c. 1908

One of a series of two- and three-story commercial buildings along West Exchange Avenue, this structure is typical of those that housed businesses that supported the stockyards. Most were built between 1906 and 1910 when the stockyards experienced rapid growth. Over the years, the ground floor of this building housed furniture stores and a dry-goods store, while the upper floors were used as a boarding house or hotel. The Stock Yards Lodge No. 1224 purchased the building in 1935 and held their meetings on the third floor while continuing to lease the space on the first two floors.

12. New Isis Theater, 2401-2403 N. Main Street, 1935

Ranchers wanted more than a place to eat, drink, and sleep when they came to do business in the stockyards. For many, it was a chance to enjoy big-city entertainment such as vaudeville or the movies. The New Isis Theater was built in 1935 to replace the Isis Theater constructed on this site in 1914. Undoubtedly, there was a great deal of appeal to this modern movie palace that older venues built to house vaudeville or silent motion pictures did not have.

Marine Commercial National Register Historic District

While North Fort Worth businesses just west of the stockyards supported those doing business there, the people who lived and worked in the area relied on the business district of the Marine community. Named for Marine Creek, which flows through the area, Marine was established in the early 1890s. Even though the community officially became part of North Fort Worth in 1902 and was annexed by Fort Worth in 1909, it retained a community function and identity separate from the commercial district near the stockyards through the 1960s.

13. Fort Worth Laundry Company, 1307 N. Main Street, 1927

The main part of this building was constructed in 1927 to house Fort Worth Laundry and Dry Cleaners, the Marine district's oldest extant business. Two other buildings, a 1926 auto garage and a 1917 blacksmith shop, were eventually incorporated into the complex. Fort Worth Laundry offered employment to many women whose husbands worked in the stockyards and meat packing plants.

14. Greines Furniture Company/Mulholland Company, 1332 N. Main Street, c. 1937

In 1905, Meyer Greines, a Jewish immigrant from Russia and his son Mose, established a small furniture store in this block. Two other Greines sons also operated businesses in the area, and a third was a physician who maintained an office two blocks away. This Moderne building owes its appearance to a circa 1937 construction project, but it is not clear whether a new building was erected or an older building remodeled. Round windows at either end of the building's second floor and recessed brickwork surrounding the doorways highlight the minimalist façade. Decorative horizontal bands of ochre brick on the second floor are now covered by paint. Greines Furniture Company operated here through the late 1980s.

15. Rose/Roseland/Marine Theater, 1438-1440 N. Main Street, 1918-1920

The first motion picture theater on the North Side, this small movie house has traditionally served the community that surrounds it. The façade was remodeled in 1920, only two years after the building was originally constructed, and its appearance is credited to Fort Worth architect L. B. Weinman. During the 1940s, the theater showed many Spanish-

language films for the Mexican-American community and was a gathering place for many neighborhood activities. Long vacant, the theater was restored in 2000 for live theater and events.

Grand Avenue National Register Historic District

The Grand Avenue Historic District is a part of North Fort Worth, a community platted in 1888 and incorporated in 1902. The area, annexed by Fort Worth in 1909 and now known as the Near North Side, sits two miles northwest of downtown Fort Worth, across the Trinity River. Grand Avenue comprises the western edge of the original subdivision of North Fort Worth where the street curves along the bluffs above the West Fork of the Trinity River. Due to its proximity to the stockyards and its beautiful vistas, Grand Avenue attracted the middle management connected with the meatpacking industry.

Originally the homes on the west side of Grand Avenue could be accessed directly from the Jacksboro Highway via long, steep drives, but now the hillside is largely overgrown with mixed vegetation. In contrast to the grandeur of the district's siting, the homes are relatively modest. The dominant house type is the wood-frame bungalow. The Grand Avenue Historic District is a remnant of the never fully realized nineteenth-century design for the planned suburb of North Fort Worth and a product of the early-twentieth-century growth of the city around its burgeoning North Side stockyards and meatpacking industry.

16. Whalen-Jary House, 1505 Grand Avenue, 1914

This substantial home was built for Joseph L. Whalen, a restaurateur, but purchased in 1919 by William E. Jary, a manager for the George W. Saunders Commission Company in the stockyards. The most distinctive part of this stucco-and-brick home is the Alamo Revival parapet on the front portico that features a single cast-stone star.

17. House, 1701 Grand Avenue,
c. 1910

The Shingle Style, where shingles sheath the entire house, is extremely rare in Fort Worth. Although it currently has a modern asphalt shingle roof, the rest of the home – including

the square porch columns – is clad in wooden shingles. The house is also set off from its neighbors by its distinctive siting at a forty-five-degree angle to the street.

18. Armstrong House, 1725 Grand Avenue, 1904

One of the earliest houses in the district, the Armstrong House was home to William L. Armstrong, a bookkeeper. The large two-story frame house has a curved, wraparound porch that provides a superb view from the Grand Avenue bluffs.

19. Waddy R. Ross House, 1352 Park Street, 1917

Waddy Ross was a self-made millionaire who, with his brothers, operated the Ross Brothers Horse and Mule Company in the stockyards. The brothers made a fortune selling horses and mules to the United States government during both world wars, and Ross was at one time the world's leading horse and mule dealer. This house, which forms the northern end of the Grand Avenue Historic District, is the largest and grandest house on the North Side. While other livestock entrepreneurs chose to live on the South or West sides of Fort Worth rather than in close proximity to the smells of the stockyards and packing plants, Ross chose to live near the industry that helped him build his empire.

Fort Worth–South Side

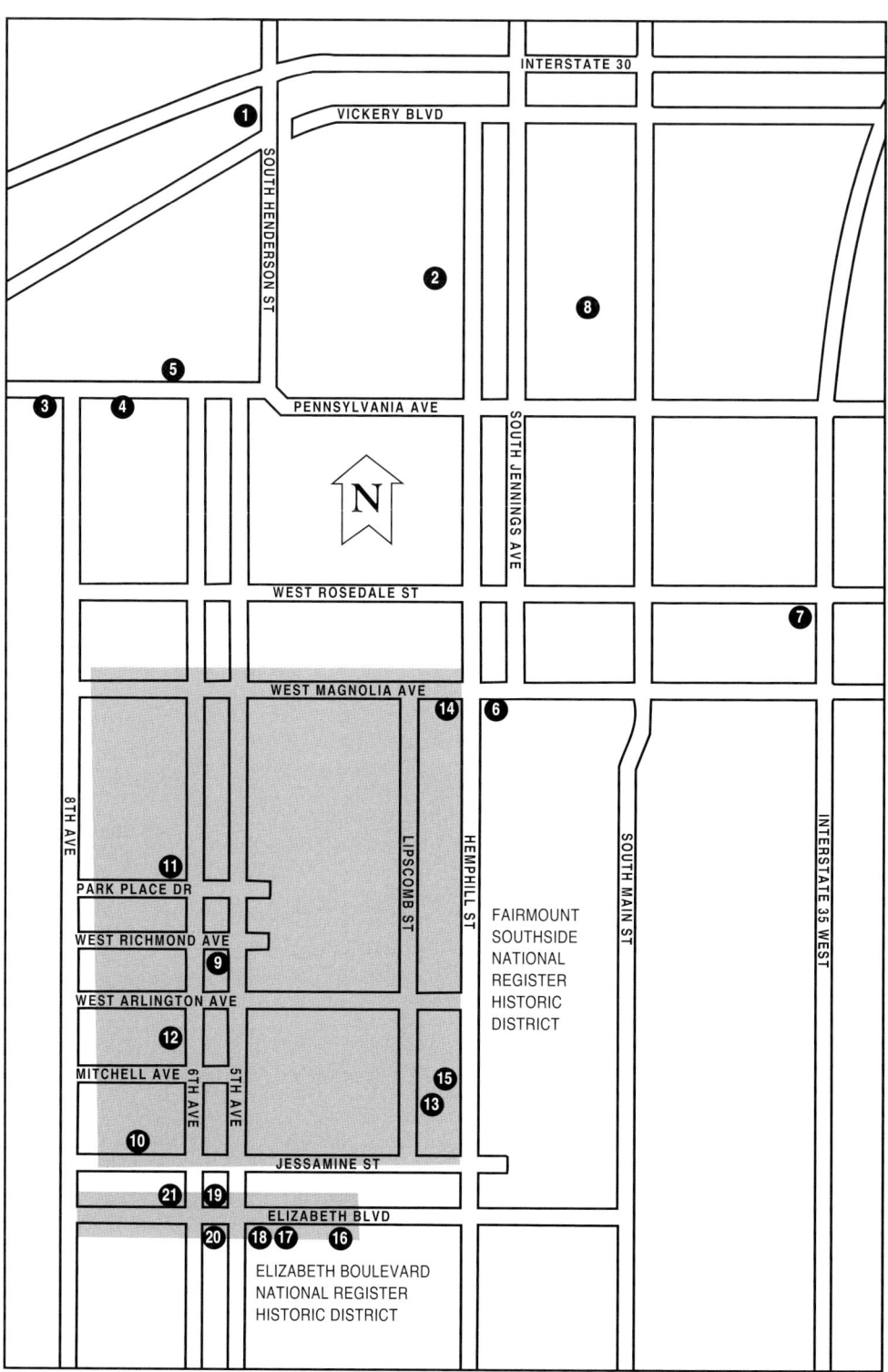

Fort Worth–South Side

As Fort Worth began to grow outside of the original town site, it first grew west towards the Trinity River and then south. The area just west of downtown but east of the Trinity River was small and largely built up by the 1890s. Although there was some growth to the north, the high bluff of the Trinity River made transportation difficult until a good bridge was built. The same problem also slowed growth to the east and west. To the south, there were no natural barriers that would slow development, and people began to move south of the Texas & Pacific Railway tracks shortly after the railroad arrived in 1876. By the mid-1880s, there was substantial development in the section of the South Side located north of Pennsylvania Avenue – an area that was within reasonable walking distance of the central business district. Most of these houses have been

---

Map: South Side

1. Public Market Building
2. Stephen F. Austin Elementary School/Williamson-Dickie Manufacturing Co.
3. Mitchell-Schoonover House
4. Thistle Hill
5. Woman's Club Buildings
6. Saint Mary of the Assumption Catholic Church
7. James E. Guinn School
8. Beth El Congregation

Fairmount Southside National Register Historic District
9. Darnall House
10. Jordan-Edelman House
11. Benton House
12. Martin-Campbell House
13. Huffman House
14. Modern Drug
15. Reeves-Walker House

Elizabeth Boulevard National Register Historic District
16. Dulaney House
17. Sparks House
18. Hoffer-Hulen House
19. Ryan-Smith House
20. Smith House
21. Fuller-Snyder House

replaced by industrial and medical facilities. Other developments were planned, but little construction occurred until streetcar routes and city services were extended south of downtown. The economic boom brought by the establishment of the Armour and Swift meatpacking plants also spurred South Side development. Most of the existing historic South Side residential neighborhoods were built up between 1905 and the Great Depression of the 1930s, and by World War II almost all of the South Side was developed.

1. Public Market Building, 1400 Henderson Street, 1930 (NR & RTHL)

Oklahoma City developer John J. Harden had this commercial structure built in 1930 to provide market space for local farmers, vendors, and retail businesses. Similar to another Harden market project in Oklahoma City, it features influences of the Spanish Colonial Revival, Italian Baroque Revival, and Art Deco styles. Retail businesses were housed in the main building, while farmers sold produce from the shed building that wraps around the back of the main market. The market remained in operation until 1941 and the building later housed a variety of businesses. During the early 1980s, the Public Market Building was threatened with demolition to facilitate expansion of the Interstate 30 freeway, but National Register designation and a lawsuit forced the Texas Department of Transportation to look for alternative routes and the building was spared.

2. Stephen F. Austin Elementary School/Williamson-Dickie Manufacturing Co. Headquarters, 319 Lipscomb Street, 1892, 1909, 1958 (NR)

Originally built as the Sixth Ward School, this attractive Romanesque Revival building is one of the oldest standing school buildings in Tarrant County. Local architects Messer, Sanguinet and Messer designed the building, which was constructed in 1892 as Fort Worth grew beyond the boundaries of the central business district by "jumping" the Texas & Pacific Railway track on the southern end of town. Renamed Stephen F. Austin

Elementary School in 1904, in honor of the revolutionary hero who helped colonize Texas, the building was expanded as Fort Worth's South Side residential neighborhoods grew. Despite changing architectural trends, the 1909 addition uses the large stone arches that define the Romanesque Revival style. Over the years, the character of this neighborhood became more commercial than residential, and the school closed in 1977. It has served since 1980 as offices for the Williamson-Dickie Manufacturing Company, an apparel manufacturer.

3. Mitchell-Schoonover House, 600 8th Avenue, 1907, (RTHL)

James E. Mitchell, a jeweler, demanded a high degree of skilled craftsmanship in the construction of this house. Completed in 1907, it was designed by the Fort Worth architectural firm of Sanguinet and Staats. A friend, Dr. Charles B. Simmons, purchased the property in 1920. Ownership of the home was transferred to his daughter Maurine and her husband Dr. Frank Schoonover in 1945. They occupied the residence until 1979.

4. Thistle Hill / Wharton-Scott House, 1509 Pennsylvania Avenue, 1903 (NR & RTHL)

Thistle Hill is probably Fort Worth's most imposing cattle-baron mansion. Built in 1902 as a "honeymoon cottage" for Electra Waggoner, daughter of ranching magnate W. T. Waggoner, and her husband Albert B. Wharton, the home served as a center for their lavish social life. In 1911, the Whartons moved to their ranch land and sold the house to Elizabeth and Winfield Scott. Scott, who made his fortune in ranching and real estate development, decided to remodel the house and hired the original architects, Sanguinet and Staats, to remove the less formal Colonial Revival detailing and substitute more formal Georgian Revival-style elements. The massive limestone columns, green tile roof, and small wrought-iron balcony all date from this period. Scott died before he could move into the house, but his wife and son lived here through the 1930s. After his mother's death, Winfield Scott, Jr., sold most of the home's fur-

nishings and finally the house itself. Between 1940 and 1968, the Girls Service League provided housing for working women in the home. Although alterations were made, Thistle Hill survived a period when many of Fort Worth's other cattle-baron mansions were demolished for commercial development. Grassroots efforts by the Save-the-Scott-Home group raised funds to purchase and restore the house in 1976, and it was opened as a historic house museum as the restoration process progressed. Now restored, Thistle Hill is open for tours, and the home may be rented for weddings and other events.

5. Woman's Club Buildings, 1300 block, Pennsylvania Avenue (OTHM)

Women from eleven social and study groups, some formed before 1900, joined in 1923 to create the Woman's Club of Fort Worth. Miss Anna Shelton, who led the unification drive, served as the first president. The charter members first met in a house donated by Etta O. (Mrs. William G.) Newby. As the club grew, it acquired and built other buildings along the block. Over the years, the complex of four historic homes and three newer structures was landscaped and painted to present a unified appearance. The organization offers many civic, charitable, and educational activities and maintains a Texana library collection.

6. Saint Mary of the Assumption Catholic Church, 501 W. Magnolia, 1924 (NR)

St. Mary of the Assumption Church is a Romanesque Revival structure built of mottled red brick with limestone trim. It was the fourth Catholic parish established in Fort Worth, built to serve the spiritual needs of the city's rapidly growing South Side. After a wooden church was destroyed by fire in 1922, members decided to rebuild on the same site and selected the firm of Sanguinet, Staats and Hedrick to design this building. The Carrara marble altar and sculptures of Jesus, Joseph, and Mary, rescued when the frame church burned, were installed in the new building. Saint Mary's continues to serve as a neighborhood parish church.

7. James E. Guinn School, 1150 South Freeway, 1927, 1937, 1953-1954 (NR & OTHM)

The James E. Guinn School is a complex of three buildings grouped together at the southwestern corner of Rosedale and I-35W, the South Freeway. It includes the elementary school building designed by Wiley G. Clarkson and built in 1927, the junior high building designed by the Elmer G. Withers Architectural Company and built in 1937, and the gymnasium/shop building designed by Wyatt C. Hedrick and built in 1953-1954. Named for James Elvis Guinn, a Fort Worth native and principal of the South Side Colored School that served the neighborhood before this complex was built, this school played a major role in educating African-American children during segregation. It was the largest black school in Fort

Worth in 1930, serving approximately twelve hundred students annually. The complex stood vacant for many years after the school closed in 1980, but the Fort Worth Business Assistance Center now occupies the middle school building and there are plans for a Med Tech Center in the gymnasium.

8. Beth-El Congregation, 207 W. Broadway (OTHM)

Fort Worth's first Reform synagogue, Beth-El Congregation, was formed in 1902 with forty-three members. Sam Levy, a wealthy cigar and liquor dealer, was the temple's first president. The early days of the congregation were difficult ones, and for a time services were held sporadically. Student rabbis from Hebrew Union College in Cincinnati conducted services for High Holy Days. The first rabbi was hired in 1904, and in 1907 the congregation purchased a lot on the corner of Fifth and Taylor streets in downtown Fort Worth, completing its first temple building in 1908. By 1920 the congregation had outgrown the downtown building and moved into a new red-brick temple on Fort Worth's South Side that fall. Despite a major fire in 1946, the Broadway building served the congregation until 2000 when a new temple located at 4900 Briarhaven Road, just off Hulen Street near Congregation Ahavath Sholom, was completed. Cast-stone menorah from the front of the old building, the historical subject marker, and other items were moved to the new synagogue.

Fairmount/Southside National Register Historic District

The Fairmount/Southside Historic District is a large, early-twentieth-century neighborhood on Fort Worth's the near South Side, approximately two miles south of downtown. Although the district includes parts of twenty-two subdivisions, the core area has a consistent, unified feeling with blocks of modest houses set closely behind small front yards. Fairmount was developed as a middle-class residential area between 1890 and 1938, with the largest concentration of houses dating from 1905 to 1920. Wood-frame bungalows and variations on the two-story, four-square form are the most common styles. Fairmount's grander homes are concentrated in the eastern sections of the district. Chase Court, a private, deed-restricted street, contains a small pocket of these finer homes within a distinct streetscape. The district also includes many early-twentieth-century commercial buildings, which were developed along the streetcar lines. The streetcar made possible accelerated development of the South Side after 1900 when Fort Worth

was experiencing another growth spurt due to the establishment of the meat-packing industry.

9. Darnall House, 1908 Fifth Avenue, 1909

The most distinctive part of this charming one-story wood-frame cottage is the fully shingled porch recessed beneath the gable slope of the roof. The house was built by a real estate developer as a speculative property and sold to Emma Darnall, a widow.

10. Jordan-Edelman House, 2263 Fairmount Avenue, c. 1920-1921

After World War I, a variation on the bungalow form developed, popularly known as the airplane bungalow. The cross-gabled roof is wide and shallow, creating wing-like extensions off the main body of the house, while a small single-room second story rises like a cockpit from the central block of the house. Robert Jordan, an oilman, and Samuel Edelman, a jeweler, were the first two owners of this home.

11. Benton House, 1730 Sixth Avenue, 1900 (NR individual listing& RTHL)

One of the oldest houses in this historic district, the Benton House is Fort Worth's best example of a Queen Anne cottage. It was built for tobacco salesman Meredith A. Benton and his wife, Ella Belle. Family accounts tell of Mrs. Benton watching her husband leave the old T & P Railway Station and cross the open prairie in a horse and buggy as he made his way home after a trip. Architecturally, its wraparound porch distinguishes the home as does the ornate Eastlake trim, one of the largest concentrations of Victorian gingerbread detailing in the city. When it was first built, the house had a barn with a hayloft and two-room servants' house on the west side of the lot, but they were replaced by the current garage building 1937. The fence that surrounds the double lot is largely original, and the home is still owned by Benton family descendents. In addition to being part of the Fairmount/Southside Historic District, the Benton House is also individually listed on the National Register for its architectural qualities.

12. *Martin-Campbell House, 2108 Sixth Avenue, c. 1915*

This distinctive bungalow, constructed of fieldstone and clinker brick (brick that has been over-fired to produce twisted or deformed shapes with glazed surfaces), is one of the best examples of this style in the Fairmount/Southside Historic District. The open timber trusses in the porch gable and the narrow, vertical windows add to the home's charm. The house was built about 1915 for Julia Martin, widow of Sidney Martin, former president of Martin-Brown Mercantile Company.

13. *Huffman House, 2223 Lipscomb Street, 1919-1920*

Master stonemason James B. Huffman built this house of Indiana gray limestone as his own residence in 1919-1920. Huffman owned a stone yard near Pioneers Rest Cemetery and handled the stonework for a number of public buildings in Texas. His 1923 obituary noted that Huffman "operated one of the largest stone-cutting plants in Texas." The house is built of stone, not stone veneer over a wooden frame, and demonstrates his mastery of stone work and stone carving. Huffman also built the house next door, at 2221 Lipscomb, and lived there for a few years before building his final tour de force.

14. Modern Drug, 1300 Hemphill Street, 1927

Prominently sited on the corner of Hemphill and Magnolia, this building housed La Cava Cleaners and Modern Drugs for many years. It is typical of the one- and two-story commercial buildings that lined the commercial thoroughfares surrounding the Fairmount/Southside residential neighborhood. The building has recently been renovated to house a bank on the ground floor, with loft apartments upstairs.

15. Reeves-Walker House, 2200 Hemphill Street, 1907-1908 (RTHL)

William Reeves, who ran private banking and brokerage businesses, chose what was by then an outdated style when he built this classically detailed Queen Anne home in 1907-1908. Still, it was appropriate for a man who wanted to reassure his clients that a solid and stable individual managed their money. A 1914 sketch described this large and impressive residence as "one of the handsomest homes in Texas." By the 1960s, the character of Hemphill Street was changing from residential to commercial and the family of the second owners, Myrtle and John L. Walker, a grain dealer, sold the house for use as a funeral home. Today, it serves as a law office.

Elizabeth Boulevard National Register Historic District

Elizabeth Boulevard, named for the wife of developer John C. Ryan, was designed as the first phase of a restricted residential district known as Ryan Place and platted in 1911. Locally prominent architects and builders produced the city's most exuberant examples of the various eclectic and revival styles here. Elizabeth Boulevard's design followed the tenets of the City Beautiful Movement, which held that planned development based on classical architectural styles and extensive street landscaping would create a pleasant, urban, park-like neighborhood. The exclusive area was the home of many prominent Fort Worth oilmen and business leaders. Elizabeth Boulevard was Fort Worth's first residential historic district. It was listed on the National Register in 1979.

16. Dulaney House, 1001 Elizabeth Boulevard, 1923

The most romantic of a handful of Mediterranean Revival style houses on Elizabeth Boulevard, this home was built for oilman Richard Otto

Dulaney, owner of the Planet Petroleum Company. Architect Raphael A. Nicolais designed extensive terra cotta ornamentation for the brick residence, including columns and eave brackets, that give it a fanciful air. Dulaney also built the Sinclair Building in downtown Fort Worth.

17. Sparks House, 1215 Elizabeth Boulevard, 1912

The only wood-frame house on Elizabeth Boulevard, this residence was built in 1912 for John Sparks, president of Stockyards National Bank. John C. Ryan stipulated masonry for all structures in this restricted subdivision, but made an exception for his friend Sparks. It was the second house built on the boulevard.

18. Hoffer-Hulen House, 1221 Elizabeth Boulevard, 1922

Designed by Fort Worth architect Wiley G. Clarkson, this two-story, Renaissance Revival style home was built in 1922 for oilman Temple B.

Hoffer. It is better remembered, however, as the home of Major General John A. Hulen, commander of the 36th Division, United States Army, during World War I, and later president of the Fort Worth & Denver City Railway. Hulen Street, a major north-south artery on Fort Worth's near-west side, is named for the general.

19. Ryan-Smith House, 1302 Elizabeth Boulevard, 1915

John C. Ryan chose to build his own home in Ryan Place, a testament to the qualities of his exclusive development. Built in 1915, the two-story, formal Italian Renaissance Revival style home was designed by the Fort Worth architectural firm of Field and Clarkson and constructed in tan brick with a green ceramic tile roof at a cost of just under $20,000. Grain dealer Bert K. Smith, co-owner of the Smith Brothers Grain Company with his brother Jule, bought the house in 1918, about the time his brother built a home just down the block at 1315 Elizabeth Boulevard. The house remained in the Smith family until 1965.

20. Smith House, 1315 Elizabeth Boulevard, 1918

Architect Wiley G. Clarkson designed this home for Jule G. Smith just down the street from his brother's residence. The graceful two-story, tile-and-stucco home has a full terrace across the front façade and a central entry flanked by Palladian windows. The house remained in the Smith family until 1972.

21. Fuller-Snyder House, 1400 Elizabeth Boulevard, 1923

This fine stuccoed example of the Spanish Colonial Revival style was built for William Marshall Fuller, a cottonseed products dealer. Sited on a corner lot, the home has an almost theatrical presence with its arcaded portico on the southeast corner, wrought iron balcony, stained glass window, and elaborate arched entryway. Later owners of the home were Susie and D. H. Snyder, a ranching family.

Fort Worth–West Side

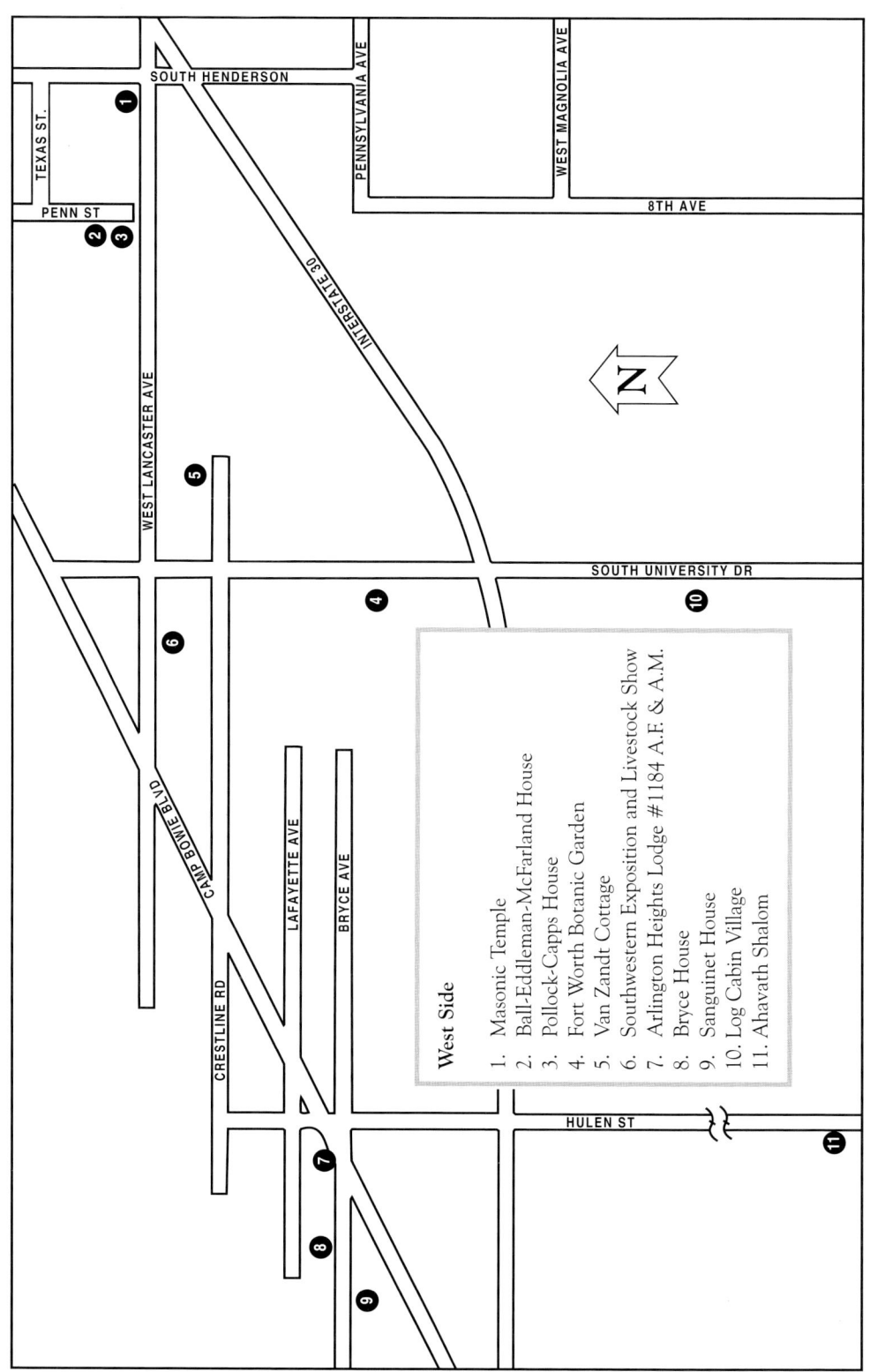

Fort Worth–West Side

During the early years, the Trinity River slowed Fort Worth's westward development, and 1880s residences perched on the bluff overlooking the river, just west of the central business district. There were farms west of the Trinity but little other development. Arlington Heights, one of Fort Worth's first suburbs, was platted in 1890 as an exclusive residential area linked to the city by a streetcar line that ran down the median of what is now Camp Bowie Boulevard. The Panic of 1893 and the resulting financial depression led to the bankruptcy of the Chamberlain Development Company, halting construction for several years. During World War I, the United States Army established a military training field here, in part because of the existing streetcar line, and development flourished after the army left. Closer to town, but still west of the Trinity, the old Van Zandt farm was transformed in 1936 to host the Frontier Centennial Exposition celebrating the centennial of Texas independence. Today the area thrives as the Cultural District, home to the Southwestern Exposition and Livestock Show and museums.

1. *Masonic Temple, 1100 Henderson Street, 1930-1932 (RTHL)*

Masonic organizations have been active in Fort Worth since 1854. By the 1920s, there were several downtown-area lodges, and meeting space was crowded. This building was intended to provide a single meeting place for all member bodies. Designed by Fort Worth architect Wiley G. Clarkson and completed in 1932, the temple is a blend of Neo-classical and Art Moderne styling. As befits Masonic tradition, the building sits on an elevated site and faces east. It is a stepped-back temple-form structure with massive Ionic columns on the top floor. Masonic emblems, decorative metal grilles, and dramatic stainless-steel front door panels depicting the three Masters of Masonry who helped build King Solomon's temple enliven this imposing and somewhat austere building.

2. Ball-Eddleman-McFarland House, 1110 Penn Street, 1899 (NR & RTHL)

Designed by Howard Messer, this Queen Anne-style house was built in 1899 for Sarah C. Ball, widow of the wealthy Galveston banker George Ball, at a cost of $38,000. The house overlooks downtown Fort Worth, facing to the east, and is located in an area known as Quality Hill. Fort Worth's cattlemen, bankers, and professional people lived in this exclusive residential area during the boom period of the Fort Worth cattle industry in the first decades of the twentieth century. William H. Eddleman, a local banker, bought the home in 1904 and moved here with his wife and their daughter and her husband. In 1921 Eddleman gave the house to his daughter Caroline, wife of cattleman Frank H. McFarland. Mrs. McFarland lived here for seventy-five years, until her death in 1978. Her decision to live in the house at a time when many of her neighbors were moving helped preserve it as one of only a handful of cattle-baron mansions left in this neighborhood. The exterior features five chimneys, elaborate brick-and-sandstone detailing, a slate roof, and decorative copper flashings and finials. Inside, the floors in each room have a different inlaid parquet design with many types of hardwood arranged in a variety of star, leaf, and geometric patterns. Historic Fort Worth, Inc. now offers tours of the home, which may also be rented for meetings and special events.

3. Pollock-Capps House, 1120 Penn Street, 1898 (NR & RTHL)

Built in 1898 for homeopathic physician Dr. Joseph R. Pollock, this mansion was sold to attorney, real estate developer, and newspaper publisher William Capps and his wife Sallie whose family lived here from 1910 until 1971. William Capps remodeled the house in 1910 by enlarging and rebuilding the  porch and adding two bedrooms, another bath, and a conservatory. The grounds at one time included a barn for horses and cows, a three-car garage with ballroom above, a golf course, and a tennis court. In the days before air conditioning, the bluff-top lots along Penn Street were prime real estate because homes built here caught the cooling breezes. Like its next door neighbor, the Ball-Eddleman-McFarland House, the Pollock-Capps House is one of Fort Worth's hallmark Victorian residences. The home has been used for offices since the early 1970s.

4. Mary Daggett Lake/Fort Worth Botanic Garden, 3220 Rock Springs Road (OTHM)

Garden clubs were one of the civilizing influences as frontier towns grew into cities. Fort Worth native Mary Daggett Lake played a prominent role in the civic life of her hometown through her work as a writer for the *Fort Worth Star-Telegram* and leadership roles with the Fort Worth Garden Club and the Board of Park Commissioners. In 1907, city planner George

Kessler recommended that the Rock Springs area be purchased and used as a city park. The land was acquired in 1912, but little development took place until 1930 when landscape architect S. Herbert Hare drew plans for the garden. Funds for construction came from the park board and federal work relief funds. Seven hundred and fifty out-of-work stonemasons and apprentices were hired to build the rose garden, lagoon, and other structures, and the garden was dedicated in October 1933. Lake and the Fort Worth Garden Club established the state's first garden center here in 1935 in a stone building along the main drive near the center of the garden complex. Today, the building houses a library holding Mrs. Lake's papers and a restaurant. Also a historian, Mrs. Lake edited the first edition of this guide, published in 1949. The Fort Worth Botanic Garden is still a favorite place for weddings, family reunions, picnics, or quiet walks.

5. Van Zandt Cottage, 2900 Crestline Road, c. 1870 (RTHL)

Built about 1870 on the road to Weatherford, this cottage is reputedly the oldest cabin in Fort Worth still standing on its original site. Khleber Miller Van Zandt, who came to Fort Worth in 1865, became involved in banking, retail merchandising, newspapers, and the cattle business, as well as many civic activities, and was known as "Mr. Fort Worth." He bought the cottage at auction to settle unpaid debts owed to his mother by the previous owners, Sarah M. and George Scoggins. It is not clear whether Van Zandt and his family lived here, but they had significant land holdings in the vicinity, and family sources place them at the cottage between

about 1871 and 1878. When plans were being made to celebrate the 1936 Texas Centennial, a group of women decided to restore the cottage and open it to the public during the festivities. They hired architect Joseph R. Pelich and, with assistance from the Julia Jackson Chapter No. 141 of the Daughters of the Confederacy and the Daughters of the Republic of Texas, undertook what was probably Fort Worth's first historic preservation project.

6. Southwestern Exposition and Livestock Show, 3300 Crestline Road (OTHM)

Fort Worth's livestock show began in 1896 on the banks of Marine Creek in North Fort Worth. Intended to promote the production and sale of quality animals, over the years the stock show has grown to include a rodeo, midway, and youth activities. In 1944 the show moved to the Will Rogers Memorial Center, constructed in 1936-1937 on the heels of Fort Worth's Texas Centennial activities. Although the complex has expanded dramatically, the rodeo is still housed in the coliseum, which features a unique system of arched trusses joined at the peak allowing an unobstructed interior view. The complex is named for humorist Will Rogers, a close friend of Fort Worth newspaper publisher and civic leader Amon Carter; Rogers was killed in an Alaska airplane crash in 1935. The memorial tower contains a tribute to Rogers, who is also portrayed in the 1941-1942 sculpture by Electra Waggoner Biggs on the front lawn.

7. Arlington Heights Lodge #1184 A.F. & A.M. – Fort Worth, 4600 Camp Bowie Boulevard, 1923 (RTHL)

Chartered on December 9, 1921, Arlington Heights Lodge No. 1184 is located on land donated by lodge members. The classical temple-form building was designed by lodge member J. C. Davies and dedicated on January 3, 1923. Arlington Heights experienced a period of rapid growth during the 1920s after the Camp Bowie military base was closed, and this was one of many commercial and civic structures erected along Camp Bowie Boulevard. The building occupies a triangular lot formed by the angled intersection of a residential street. This allowed the lodge to build a temple that faced east towards the point of the triangle, following Masonic practice.

8. Fairview/Bryce House, 4900 Bryce Avenue, 1893 (NR & RTHL)

A native of Scotland, William J. Bryce moved to Fort Worth in 1883 and developed a successful brick contracting business. In 1893 he constructed this house on a corner lot in Arlington Heights. The prominent architectural firm of Messer, Sanguinet and Messer designed the home. Bryce handled all of the brickwork on this imposing solid-brick dwelling and that probably

allowed him to build a more imposing residence than he could have otherwise afforded. A rare example of a Chateauesque dwelling in Texas, Fairview is designed in a style that was popular for wealthy and influential business people and features Romanesque arches, a steeply pitched roof, and distinctive gabled dormers. The mayor of Fort Worth from 1927 to 1933, Bryce lived here until his death in 1944.

9. Sanguinet House, 4729 Collinwood Avenue, 1894 (NR & RTHL)

Noted Fort Worth architect Marshall R. Sanguinet built this Shingle Style house about 1894, incorporating his earlier residence at this site that was damaged by fire. Sanguinet was one of the most successful architects in Texas during the period from 1885 to 1926. A graduate of Washington University in St. Louis, he arrived in Fort Worth in 1883. Sanguinet was a partner in a number of architectural firms prior to the formation of the firm of Sanguinet and Staats in 1903. In partnership with Carl Staats, who was trained as an engineer, Sanguinet was responsible for many important buildings in Fort Worth, in addition to work in Austin, Houston, and Shreveport, Louisiana. The two-story, masonry-and-frame house combines simple yet handsome brickwork with wood shingles in an asymmetrical composition. It is decidedly more modern in appearance than the Bryce House or other residences being built in Fort Worth at that time. Sanguinet's design for the house was clearly influenced by the Arts and Crafts Movement, and it is an important Texas example of the progressive trends in American domestic architecture at the turn-of-the-century.

10. Texas Log Cabins/Log Cabin Village, 2100 Log Cabin Village Lane (OTHM)

The log cabin, a familiar sight in Cross Timbers country of North Texas during the mid-nineteenth century, was a favored building form in areas where settlers were too far from civilization to obtain milled lumber. These seven cabins, most built during the 1850s, were gathered from Parker, Tarrant, Hood, and Milam counties, when disuse or development threatened their existence, and placed in this park setting. An early historic preservation project, Log Cabin Village was opened to the public in 1966. Included in the complex, now operated as a living history museum, are the Parker cabin, which was the home of pioneer statesman Isaac Parker and sheltered his niece, Cynthia Ann Parker, for a short time after she was taken from her Comanche family in 1860, and the Tomkins cabin, at one time a landmark on the Fort Worth-Belknap Road.

11. Congregation Ahavath Sholom, 4050 S. Hulen Street (OTHM)

Fort Worth's first Jewish congregation, Congregation Ahavath Sholom, was organized in 1892. Most of the early members were Eastern European immigrants, and the name they selected for the synagogue means, "love of peace." William Goldstein served as its first president. The first synagogue was a wooden structure built in 1893 at the corner of Hemphill and Jarvis streets on Fort Worth's South Side, in the area where many of the members lived. In 1901, the congregation moved to downtown Fort Worth and occupied a building on Taylor Street. They constructed a new temple in 1906 and a building to house the congregation's Hebrew Institute in 1915. Congregation Ahavath Sholom built their fourth temple on 8th Avenue in 1952 and worshiped there until 1980 when they moved further south to Hulen Street.

Fort Worth–Northeast and East Side

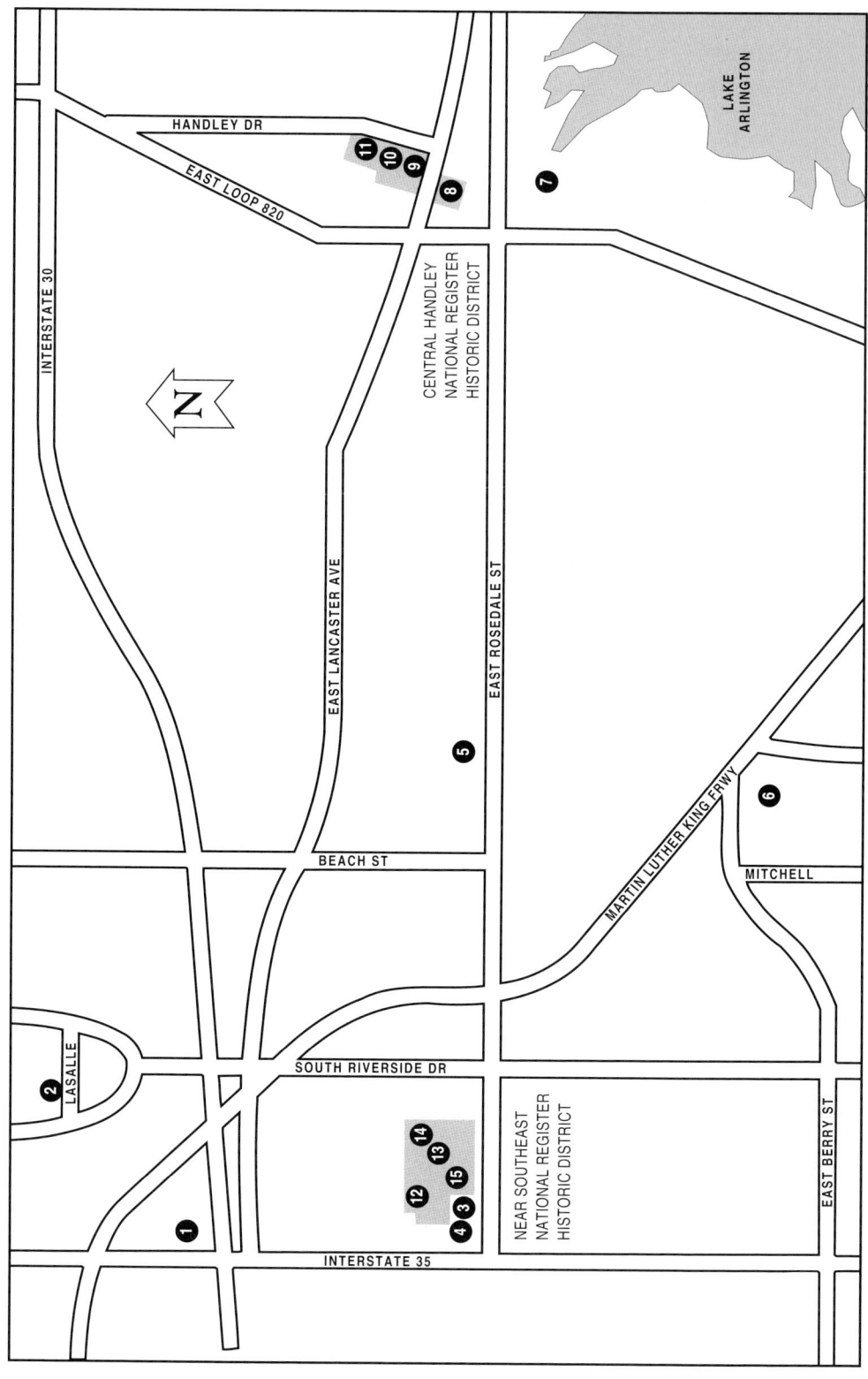

Fort Worth–Northeast and East Side

Fort Worth's historic neighborhoods on the Northeast and East sides generally developed as suburbs outside the city limits. Some, like Handley and Polytechnic Heights, had commercial centers, but all were generally residential in character. Streetcars, which allowed families without automobiles to live farther away from the town center, were essential to the development of these communities. Polytechnic Heights grew up around an old cotton mill and Polytechnic College (now Texas Wesleyan University), and Riverside was platted in 1891 by the East Fort Worth Town Company. Many of the additions making up the near Southeast neighborhood were platted during the 1890s but did not develop appreciably until after 1900. Handley was established in 1885 but saw most of its growth after the Interurban arrived in 1902. Other communities include Oakhurst, Meadowbrook, Morningside, and Stop Six, named for the sixth stop on the Interurban. Fort Worth annexed most of these areas in one of two waves of annexation in 1909 or 1922. City fathers were con-

---

Northeast and East Side

1. I. M. Terrell High School
2. Riverside Public School
3. Mount Zion Baptist Church
4. Sunshine Cumberland Presbyterian Church
5. Administration Building, Texas Wesleyan University
6. Masonic Widows and Orphans Home
7. Handley Power Plant and Lake Erie/Fort Worth-Dallas Interurban markers

Central Handley National Register Historic District
8. Handley Feed Store
9. Hubbard Drug Store/O. D. Stevens Commercial Building
10. Weiler House
11. Handley Post Office

Near Southeast National Register Historic District
12. Our Mother of Mercy Catholic Church
13. Munchus House
14. Burnett House
15. Pryor House

cerned that suburban communities were using city services without paying the full cost and prodded annexation by cutting off utilities to communities that did not agree to be annexed. Handley, which had the Interurban power plant, was not affected by this and was not annexed until 1946.

1. I. M. Terrell High School, 1411 E. 18th Street, 1909-1910, 1936-1937, 1955-1956 (OTHM)

In 1882, the Fort Worth school system opened its first free public school for African-American students, called the East Ninth Street Colored School, with educator Isaiah Milligan Terrell as a teacher and principal. Terrell served until 1915, when he became president of what is now Prairie View A&M University. Following several moves and name changes, the school was renamed I. M. Terrell High School in 1921, in honor of its former principal. In 1938, Terrell High School moved to its present location at 1411 E. 18th Street, the site of a former white elementary school. Two additions, in 1936-1937 and 1955-1956, enlarged the school. During segregation Terrell served as the only high school for African Americans in the area, and it is remembered as a place that nurtured academic achievement for minority students at a time when segregation severely limited their options. The school closed in 1973 but has recently been remodeled and currently serves as I. M. Terrell Elementary School.

2. Riverside Public School, 2629 LaSalle Street, 1911 (NR)

Riverside, now a neighborhood located approximately one-and-one-half miles north and east of the Tarrant County Courthouse, was once a separate community annexed by Fort Worth in 1922. Riverside established its own school system in 1905 with separate schools for whites and African Americans. Black students were originally taught in the Corinth Baptist Church and later in a small frame building, which was replaced by this two-room brick elementary school in 1911. Brick school buildings for African-American students were rare as the notion of "separate but equal" was rarely, if ever, equal. When the school first opened, Riverside's African-American community was extremely proud of this building. Each morning students lined up in front of the school and entered, filing either to the left or right into the classroom that was appropriate for their grade level. The room on the west side housed the lower grades, and the room for the upper grades was on the east. By the late 1920s the school was so crowded that a rented small frame building a block away housed the overflow. The school closed in 1936, replaced by a series of wood-framed cottages. Used for a time as a residence, the building now houses Corinth Baptist Church's Youth Center.

3. Mount Zion Baptist Church, 1101 Evans Avenue, 1919-1921 (RTHL)

Following the Civil War, many former slaves became Baptists because they appreciated the freedom that the denomination offered in terms of religious organization and association. Evangelist Frank Tribune established Mount Zion, a historically African-American church, in 1894 with five members. Tribune also helped organize the first South Side school for African-American children that same year in a space rented from Mount Zion. Leaving a wood-frame sanctuary at the corner of Rosedale and Louisiana, the church built this Classical Revival building between 1919 and 1921 and has worshipped here since.

4. Our Mother of Mercy Catholic Church and Parsonage/Sunshine Cumberland Presbyterian Church, 1104 Evans Avenue, c. 1929 (NR)

In 1929, the St. Joseph Society of the Sacred Heart, or "Josephites," a religious order devoted to the evangelization and spiritual needs of African Americans, helped to found Our Mother of Mercy Catholic Church. This small brick church with a corner bell tower was designed by the pastor, Father Narcissus P. Denis, and served as the congregation's first permanent home. Many members were involved in community and social service activities, and the church also operated a nearby four-room school for African-American students. The church moved to 1003 E. Terrell Avenue in 1952, and the congregation is still affiliated with the Josephites. Sunshine Cumberland Presbyterian Church purchased the building after Our Mother of Mercy moved and has made its home here since 1955.

5. Administration Building/Oneal-Sells Administration Building, Texas Wesleyan University, 1201 Wesleyan Drive, 1902-1903, 1909 (RTHL)

Polytechnic College was established in 1890 by the Northwest Texas Conference of the Methodist Episcopal Church, South, and opened for classes in 1891 on land donated by A. S. Hall, W. D. Hall, and George E. Tandy. The college retained fifty acres for the campus; the remaining two-hundred-and-fifty acres became the community of Polytechnic Heights. This building, constructed of limestone from Dublin, Texas, was built in 1902-1903 to house the college administration. The exterior owes its current classical appearance to a 1909 renovation and expansion according to plans drawn by architect M. L. Waller and modified by physics professor J. D. Boon, who also supervised construction because funds were tight.

Located at the center of the Texas Wesleyan University campus, the facility still serves as the university's administration building.

Masonic Widows and Orphans Home National Register Historic District

6. Masonic Home and School of Texas, 3600 Wichita Street, 1910-1941

The Masonic Widows and Orphans Home opened in 1899 to serve widows and orphans from throughout the state. After 1911, when the Home for Aged Masons opened in Arlington, this facility has served exclusively as a home and school for youth who are eligible relatives of Texas Masons. The twenty-six buildings that stand on the 206-acre site today generally date from the mid-1920s and were designed in a handsome rendition of the Tudor Revival style by Wiley G. Clarkson. The main buildings are laid out on a north/south axis flanking a central lawn and reached by a central road.

The visually imposing Administration Building sits at one end of the road, opposite the main entrance gates at the other end. The buildings flanking the lawn include a chapel, dormitories, a print shop, an elementary school, and a dining hall. Support buildings, from the period when the home was a working farm with 150 acres under cultivation as well as cattle and dairy operations, complete the complex.

7. Handley Power Plant and Lake Erie/Site of the Fort Worth-Dallas Interurban, 6604 E. Rosedale Street (OTHM)

The Northern Texas Traction Company originally built a power plant at this location to generate electrical power for the Fort Worth-Dallas Interurban. They also built Lake Erie to provide water for plant operations, and the area around the lake became a park that was popular for local outings and social events. Interurban rail service made it easy for people from adjacent towns to visit Lake Erie, but when the Interurban stopped operating in 1934 and the number of visitors declined, the park was closed. Texas Electric Service Company purchased the power plant in 1932 and ran it until 1956 when they built Lake Arlington, drained Lake Erie, and demolished the old plant to make way for Unit 3 of the current power plant complex. Two historical markers, one covering the Interurban and the other discussing the power plant and Lake Erie, are located at this site.

Central Handley National Register Historic District

Handley, located approximately seven miles east of downtown Fort Worth, was platted by the Texas & Pacific Railway in 1885. The community's ties to the railroad industry were strengthened in 1902 when the Northern Texas Traction Company located the Interurban's power plant and car barns nearby. Businesses in this district served not only the railroad employees and commuters but also residents and farmers throughout this rural area. Handley was named for James M. Handley, a salesman who settled in the area. Fort Worth annexed Handley in 1946, but the community retains a distinct small-town character.

8. Handley Feed Store, 6472 E. Lancaster Avenue, 1924, 1942-1950

Serving a community that, outside of its railroad-support facilities, was based on farming and agriculture, this building has housed a feed store since 1924. The simple, one-story building originally had wood siding; the metal panels were added between 1942 and 1950. Its functional design features exposed roof rafters and wooden plank floors, typical of a small-town feed store.

9. Hubbard Drug Store/O. D. Stevens Commercial Building, 6523 E. Lancaster Avenue, c. 1933

Although this building's form is typical of a 1930s-era commercial structure, it is distinguished by its materials – sandstone and petrified wood laid in framed panels and decorative ribbon patterns. Occupying a prominent location at the corner of Lancaster Avenue and Handley Drive, the building has typically housed drugstores. As significant as its appearance, however, is the buildings association with its first owner, Orley D. Stevens. Shortly after the building was completed, Stevens was convicted of robbing Handley's Texas & Pacific Railway station of $71,000 and narcotics trafficking and sentenced to twenty-seven years in Alcatraz.

10. *Weiler House, 3126 Handley Drive, c. 1906*

William and Rose Weiler moved to Handley in 1892, and he became both a successful businessman and civic leader. In addition to developing much of Handley's commercial area, Weiler also owned an insurance company, served on the school board, and promoted many public works projects. The family built this two-story, wood-frame house about 1906 and occupied it through the 1930s.

11. *Handley Post Office/Lancaster Crowley Properties, 3132 Handley Drive, 1921*

This building served as Handley's post office between 1921 and 1931, when it was replaced by a nearby structure at 3128 Handley Drive, next door to the Weiler's home. The Weilers constructed both buildings, and Rose Weiler served as postmistress through the late 1920s. During this time period it was common for post offices in small towns to be located in privately constructed buildings, and this structure also contained office space for Weiler's businesses.

Near Southeast National Register Historic District

The Near Southeast Historic District is located a few blocks east of Interstate 35 West and approximately one mile southeast of downtown Fort Worth. Containing homes generally constructed between 1900 and 1939, the district represents the core of Fort Worth's primary historic African-American residential neighborhood. Although the area was a white, working-class residential neighborhood during its early years, by 1910 African Americans began moving into the district in large numbers. William Madison McDonald, a noted African-American businessman, politician, and civic leader, played a key role in the transition. He began buying real estate here about 1910, built his own home at the corner of Terrell and Tennessee avenues, and through his bank made loans to families wanting to build in the area. Unfortunately, McDonald's residence no longer stands. By 1926 African Americans comprised the majority of the residents, and the neighborhood was home to a wide range of professional, business, and working-class families. Streetcar service, first available in this neighborhood in 1902, was also a major factor in its development. The Evans Avenue commercial district served this neighborhood but is not included in this district because of the significant changes it has undergone. With the civil rights movement of the 1950s and 1960s, many families chose to move out of the neighborhood to pursue new housing and job opportunities not available to them previously. Over the past fifty years, a large number of historic buildings in the district have been demolished, but a renewed interest in the history of the neighborhood has led to renovations and a revival.

12. Holy Name Catholic Church/Our Mother of Mercy Catholic Church, 1007 E. Terrell Avenue, 1908-1909; 1930s

This handsome Mission Revival building was originally a wood-frame church that housed the congregation of Holy Name Catholic Church. Sometime during the 1930s, stucco was applied to the building, giving it the appearance it has today. In 1952 Holy Name Church moved to a new location and Our Mother of Mercy Catholic Church, an African American congregation, relocated here from their old church home at 1104 E. Evans Avenue. The politically active congregation has continued to worship in and preserve this historic building.

13. Munchus House, 1130 E. Terrell Avenue, 1922 (RTHL)

Locally prominent black contractor George Powell constructed this Craftsman style house in 1922 for Dr. George Murry Munchus. The son of former slaves from Alabama, Munchus was founder, manager, and physician for Fort Worth's Negro Community Hospital. The Munchus home is a two-story, wood-frame residence featuring wide overhanging eaves, stick brackets, and prominent gables.

14. Burnett House, 1223 E. Terrell Avenue, 1938

This charming French Eclectic style house, unusual for Fort Worth and for the neighborhood in which it is located, was built in 1938 for Charles H. Robinson. The most prominent owners were Dr. Jesse Burnett and his wife Ethelyn. Burnett was a medical doctor who graduated from Meharry Medical College and practiced from an office in the Odd Fellows Lodge located on East Sixth Street. Ethelyn Burnett was a graduate of Wiley College.

15. Pryor House, 1064 E. Humbolt Street, c. 1915

Reverend A. W. Pryor, pastor of nearby Mount Zion Baptist Church from 1924 to 1949, purchased this bungalow-style house in 1925. Over fifty per cent of the houses in the district are bungalows, although this home is more substantial than many of the other examples.

Southeast Tarrant County

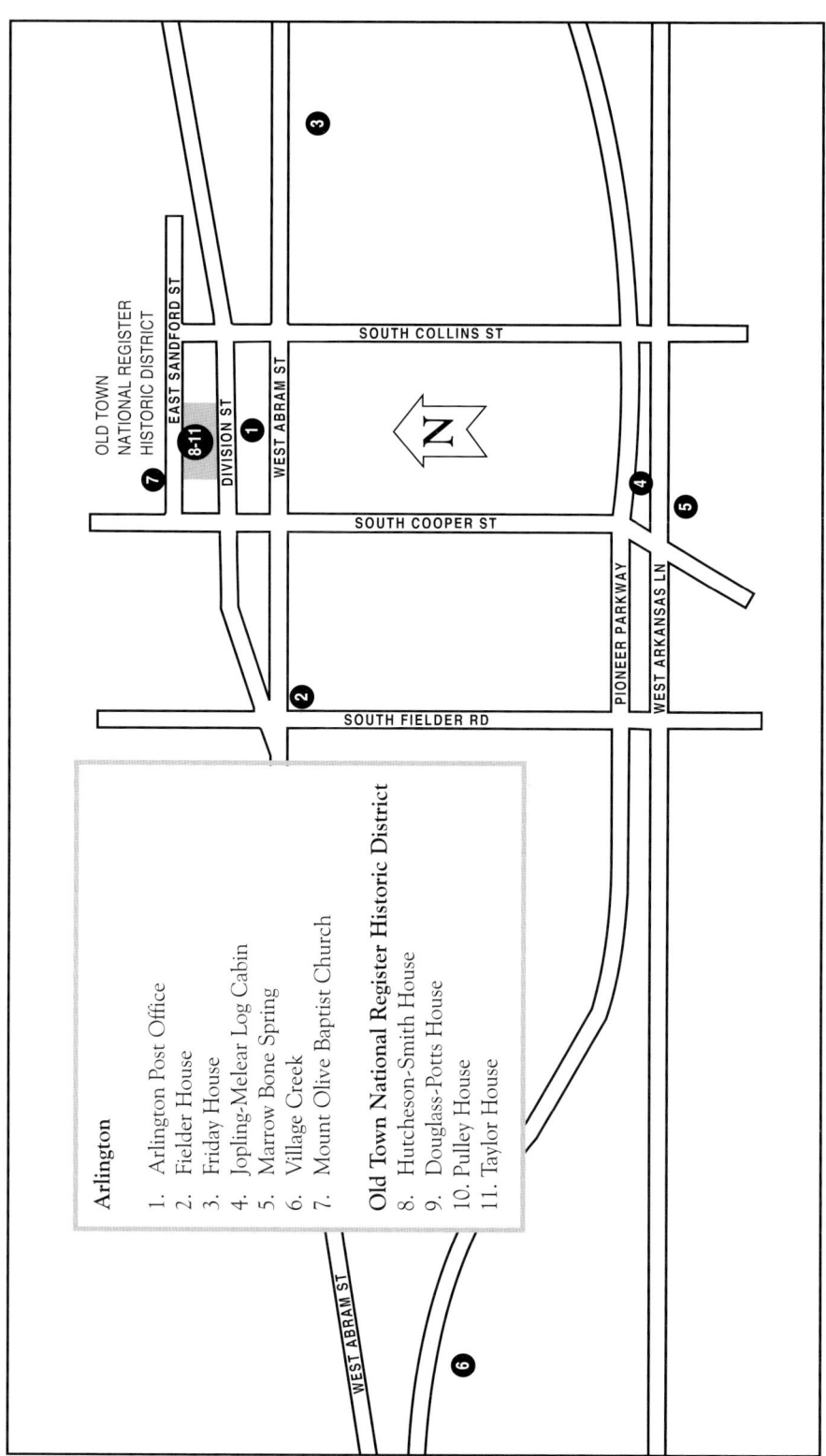

Arlington

1. Arlington Post Office
2. Fielder House
3. Friday House
4. Jopling-Melear Log Cabin
5. Marrow Bone Spring
6. Village Creek
7. Mount Olive Baptist Church

Old Town National Register Historic District

8. Hutcheson-Smith House
9. Douglass-Potts House
10. Pulley House
11. Taylor House

OLD TOWN
NATIONAL REGISTER
HISTORIC DISTRICT

EAST SANDFORD ST

DIVISION ST

WEST ABRAM ST

SOUTH COLLINS ST

SOUTH COOPER ST

SOUTH FIELDER RD

PIONEER PARKWAY

WEST ARKANSAS LN

WEST ABRAM ST

N

Southeast Tarrant County

Arlington

Arlington, named for Robert E. Lee's Virginia home, was established by the Texas & Pacific Railway in 1876 as a fueling stop on the line connecting Fort Worth and Dallas and initially served area farmers as well as railroad travelers. The Interurban, a commuter rail line linking those towns and others throughout North Texas, began running in 1902, encouraging further growth. The town's strategic location and good rail connections led many salesmen to settle their families here rather than in nearby larger communities. Education, in the form of an agricultural college that is now the University of Texas at Arlington, and defense plants established during World War II brought others here. The major boom occurred after the war when General Motors built an assembly plant in Arlington. Between 1950 and 1960, the town's population grew from 4,240 to 44,775, forever transforming the small town into a major urban community.

1. Arlington Post Office, 200 W. Main Street, 1939 (NR)

The Arlington Post Office was built from a standardized plan designed by Louis A. Simon, supervising architect for the United States Treasury

Department, who was responsible for many post office designs throughout the country. Built during the Great Depression, the Colonial Revival building features minimal detailing and straightforward form and represents the interest that President Franklin D. Roosevelt's administration had in economy and simplicity. It was Arlington's first permanent post office, as the two previous postal facilities had been housed in private commercial buildings. The post office also contains Dallas artist Otis Dozier's mural "Gathering Pecans," a reflection of small-town life in the area, an important piece from the artist's career as an American regionalist and a good example of the U. S. Treasury Department's post office mural program. This building served as Arlington's main post office until 1964 and currently houses the Worthington National Bank.

2. Fielder House, 1616 W. Abram Street, 1914 (RTHL)

Local landowner and community leader James Park Fielder and his wife Mattie erected this house in 1914. Fielder was a successful lawyer, banker, farmer, and philanthropist, who moved to Texas from Tennessee in 1884. The two-story Prairie style residence was one of the earliest brick homes in Arlington. It has a large basement used to provide storage space for the fruits and vegetables grown on the surrounding 215-acre farm. Known as "The Home on the Hill," Fielder House was a popular gathering place and a landmark for citizens of Arlington. In 1977-1978 a group of Arlington citizens successfully led a movement to preserve and restore Fielder House, and it opened in April 1980 as the Fielder Museum. Open to the public, the museum displays artifacts of Arlington and Tarrant County history.

3. Friday House, 1906 Amber's Circle, 1923 (RTHL)

In 1923, Marion and Willie Maybelle Friday purchased 112.5 acres including this site on which to build a home and pursue their love of farming. Mr. Friday was a civil engineer who built waterways and sewer systems in Dallas, Fort Worth, Arlington, and other small Texas cities. Located in East Arlington, in what was once a rural area, the four-square-plan house has classical features including a wraparound wooden porch with columns on the west and south sides and a brick porte-cochère on the north side. The home also has a concrete basement, which served both as a food storage room and a storm shelter. In 1996 the home was purchased and renovated by Liberation Community, Inc., a nonprofit housing developer.

4. Jopling-Melear Log Cabin, 621 W. Arkansas Lane, 1863 (OTHM)

George Washington Jopling erected this log cabin in 1863 in the Johnson Station community for his wife Catherine and their large family. A farmer, cattleman, and cotton gin owner, Jopling also served as a community leader and helped to organize the Johnson Station Masonic Lodge. After Catherine died Jopling remarried and deeded the cabin, which had been enlarged, to his daughter Jane Catherine and her husband Z.T. Melear, a farmer and blacksmith who owned a livery stable and cotton gin. The cabin was moved to this site in 1970, where it is now a part of a park and collection of historic buildings located near the Johnson Plantation Cemetery. Other park structures include the Watson dogtrot cabin, a one-room schoolhouse, a log barn, two Interurban stations, and the bowl from the mineral water well that once occupied the intersection of Center and Main streets in downtown Arlington.

5. Marrow Bone Spring, 600 W. Arkansas Lane (NR & OTHM)

Marrow Bone Spring, named for buffalo bones that contain rich, nourishing tissue, was used as a camping site by Native Americans for generations. Some believe that the site received its name because it was the place where Rene Robert Cavelier, Sieur de La Salle was murdered by his own men in 1687 over possession of some of the coveted bones. In 1843, a grand council held here resulted in the signing of the Treaty of Bird's Fort, the first between the Republic of Texas and ten area Indian tribes. Sam Houston designated the area as Cross Timbers Trading Post No. 1 in 1845 on land owned by Hiram Blackwell, a Peters Colony settler. Blackwell sold the land around the spring to Middleton Tate Johnson in 1852, and the village of Johnson's Station flourished nearby until the railroad arrived, following a route farther north, in 1876.

6. *Village Creek, 1516 Green Oaks Boulevard West (7th tee, Lake Arlington Golf Course) (OTHM)*

Archeological excavations along the course of this Trinity River tributary have unearthed evidence of several prehistoric villages. Artifacts from the area date back almost nine thousand years and represent a culture of food gatherers and hunters. During the 1830s the creek served as a sanctuary for several Indian tribes who made frequent raids on frontier settlements. The conflict grew worse in 1841 when major attacks were reported in Fannin and Red River counties, to the northeast along what is now the border between Texas and Oklahoma. Brigadier General Edward H. Tarrant, for whom Tarrant County is named, led a company of volunteers in a punitive expedition against Indian villages in this area. On May 24, 1841, following brief skirmishes at several encampments, two scouting patrols were attacked near the mouth of the creek and retreated to the main camp. Reportedly twelve Indians and one soldier, Captain John B. Denton, were killed. As a result of the Battle of Village Creek, many tribes began moving west. Others were later removed under terms of the 1843 Treaty of Bird's Fort, which opened the area to colonization. Much of the battle site is now located beneath the waters of Lake Arlington.

7. *Mount Olive Baptist Church, 301 W. Sanford Street (OTHM)*

A small group of African-American Tarrant County residents, led by the Rev. Mr. Squires, organized Mount Olive Baptist Church in the summer of 1897. Originally located on Indiana Street, the church moved to a new white brick sanctuary at 415 N. West Street in 1966, when the city of Arlington experienced a period of growth. The church had sixteen members in 1966, but soon the membership rolls began to increase. By 1976, when the church was formally incorporated, it had more than four hundred members. Groundbreaking for a new church building took place on October 31, 1976, and by June 1978 the members were worshiping in a new facility. A steady increase in membership led to the building of additional facilities to house the extended ministries and programs of the church. By 1986, membership totaled thirty-five hundred. The church moved to new facilities on Sanford Street near "The Hill," Arlington's historic African-American neighborhood, in 1989, and membership grew to 10,000 by 1997. In addition to its long history of providing worship and educational programs for its members, Mount Olive Baptist Church has maintained an innovative and active outreach program in the community.

Old Town National Register Historic District

The Old Town Historic District contains the nucleus of Arlington's historic housing stock. Explosive growth during the last half of the twentieth century destroyed a significant portion of the pre-World War II residential community, but these homes located in the northern portion of the original town site and three early-twentieth-century additions give a good idea of the former character of the small town.

8. Hutcheson-Smith House, 312 N. Oak Street, c. 1896 (NR individual listing & RTHL)

The most substantial home from the Victorian era still standing in Arlington, the Hutcheson-Smith house is a one-and-one-half-story frame structure with elaborate Queen Anne jigsawn trim. Located on a corner lot in the original Arlington town site, the house was probably built by I. L. Hutcheson, one of the town's founders, for his son and partner in the mercantile business, William T. Hutcheson. In 1919, S. T. Smith, a former educator and farmer, and his wife Sue purchased the home; it remained in the family until the late 1970s.

9. Douglass-Potts House, 206 W. North Street, 1907 (RTHL)

Constructed by noted local contractor Joe O. Crowley, this home is a good example of an L-plan vernacular residence, a form that was common

in North Texas during the first decade of the twentieth century. Simple in comparison with Victorian era residences such as the Hutcheson-Smith House nearby, this classic form was a forerunner of more modern house forms such as the bungalow and a reaction to the ornate decoration on nineteenth-century homes. This house was built for Wilson M. "Bud" and Clara Douglass. He was the Arlington city marshal and later the town's chief of police. W. A. and Clara Potts purchased the home in 1919, and it remained in their family until 1987.

10. Pulley House, 201 E. North Street, 1921

This home was built for W. J. and Nannie Pulley. He was a salesman for Rogers & McKnight, and she was Arlington's first telephone operator. The home's horizontal lines, broad overhanging eaves, and boxed tapered columns on brick piers are all hallmarks of Prairie School influence.

11. Taylor House, 431 N. Mesquite Street, 1922

Many of Arlington's historic residences are bungalows built during the 1910s and 1920s, a period when the town was experiencing growth due to the ease of travel on the Interurban and the presence of Grubbs Vocational College, an agricultural school which opened in 1917 and eventually became the University of Texas at Arlington. This Craftsman bungalow was built for Elmer L. Taylor. The popularity of bungalow residences marks the trend away from larger homes built at the turn of the century to more modest, practical dwellings.

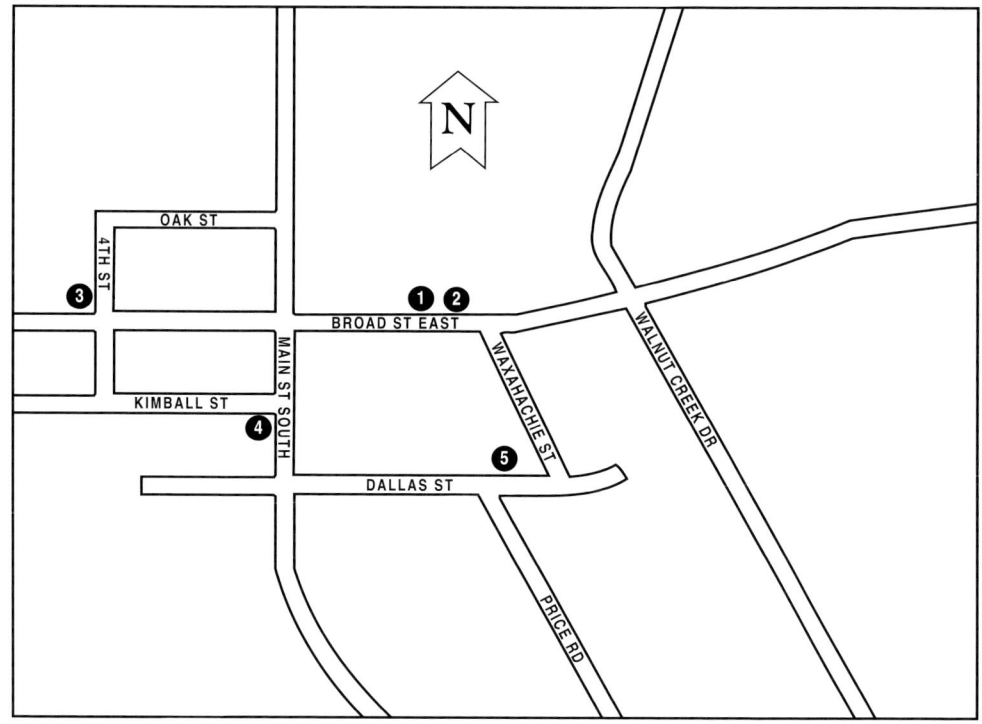

Mansfield

1. Buchanan-Hayter-Witherspoon House
2. Bratton House
3. Man House
4. Wallace-Hall House
5. Nugent-Hart House

Mansfield

Mansfield was established by Ralph S. Man and Julian B. Feild, who built a steam-powered grist mill about sixteen miles southeast of Fort Worth around 1857. The town that grew up around the mill prospered as the hub of this farming region but remained a distinctly rural community through the first half of the twentieth century. During the 1970s, Mansfield was transformed into a modern suburb, home to many who worked in Fort Worth, Arlington, or Dallas. The town's historic core retains a number of turn-of-the-century residences, a reminder of its rural past.

1. Buchanan-Hayter-Witherspoon House, 306 E. Broad Street, c. 1871; c. 1898 (NR)

This circa 1871 dwelling was originally built as a two-room structure with a center hall or passage. This was a common and practical type of house for many early settlers because it provided a covered hallway between the two rooms with front and rear doors that could be opened for ventilation. By 1898, the house had a small kitchen added to the rear and a porch with elaborate Queen Anne detailing, making it appear much more stylish than its folk origins would suggest. The house had at least seventeen owners since it was built for Thomas and R. A. Buchanan. Subsequent renovations over the years added more space to the rear of the home to accommodate growing families. As with the phased enlargement of other Mansfield homes, this practice reflected changing tastes, budgets, and advancing technology.

2. Bratton House, 310 E. Broad Street, 1895; 1910 (NR)

Andrew "Cap" Bratton, a furniture maker and undertaker, built this home for himself and his wife Emma in 1895. About 1910 the Brattons took advantage of continuing local prosperity and updated and enlarged their home. Cap Bratton removed the Queen Anne fretwork from the front porch and added a Craftsman style porch with brick piers and tapered posts. Bratton died in 1938, and in 1942 Emma Bratton, having no children,

deeded the house to her sister who was eleven years younger. The sister died in 1950, but Emma Bratton lived until 1955 when she died at the age of ninety-six. During the 1980s the house was used for commercial purposes but returned to residential use in the mid-1990s.

3. Man House, 604 W. Broad Street, c. 1865-1868 (NR & OTHM)

Ralph Sandiford Man is considered the "Father of Mansfield" because, unlike Julian Feild who moved to Fort Worth, he lived and worked here until his death in 1906. In 1863, Man married Julia Alice Boisseau, and in 1865 the couple bought 368 acres of land from Feild on which to build their home. The core of this house is a log cabin constructed about 1865, but the residence was enlarged with a brick and wood addition and the cabin covered with wooden siding in 1868. Mansfield's oldest known surviving building, this one-and-one-half story home is an eclectic design featuring Greek Revival, Colonial Revival, and Queen Ann details. The house remained in the Man family until 1946. It currently sits on a plot just under ten acres; the other portions of the original parcel were sold of through the years as Mansfield grew.

4. Wallace-Hall House, 210 S. Main Street, c. 1878 (NR)

Built about 1878, the Wallace-Hall house is a good local example of the Queen Anne style, with decorative brackets on the cut-away bays. It was the only house on this block until the land was subdivided in 1942. Located near the south end of Mansfield's primary north-south street, the house was built for James H. Wallace, a physician, and his wife Mary Ann. Dr. Wallace was perhaps more famous in death than in life. Involved in a feud with Lemuel Stephens, a relative by marriage, Wallace confronted Stephens, called him a cattle rustler, and shot him. Stephens survived, but his son then shot Wallace who died a week later. Wallace's widow lived here until 1939, and in 1942 her heirs sold the home to Lee and Marjorie Hall who operated Hall's Service Station. It remains in the Hall family, having been owned by only two families during its 125-year history.

5. Nugent-Hart House, 312 S. Waxahachie Street, c. 1892-1893 (RTHL)

In the early 1890s teacher Joseph Nugent and his wife, Christina, built this house, which features late-nineteenth-century Victorian and Eastlake details in the porch. Nugent, a native of Canada, came to Texas in 1851. He operated a private school in Mansfield during the 1850s, taught at the Mansfield Male and Female College (one of the first co-educational colleges in the state which operated from 1867 until 1889), and was elected the town's first mayor following Mansfield's incorporation in 1890. Local farmer J. H. Hart bought the home in 1920.

Northeast Tarrant County

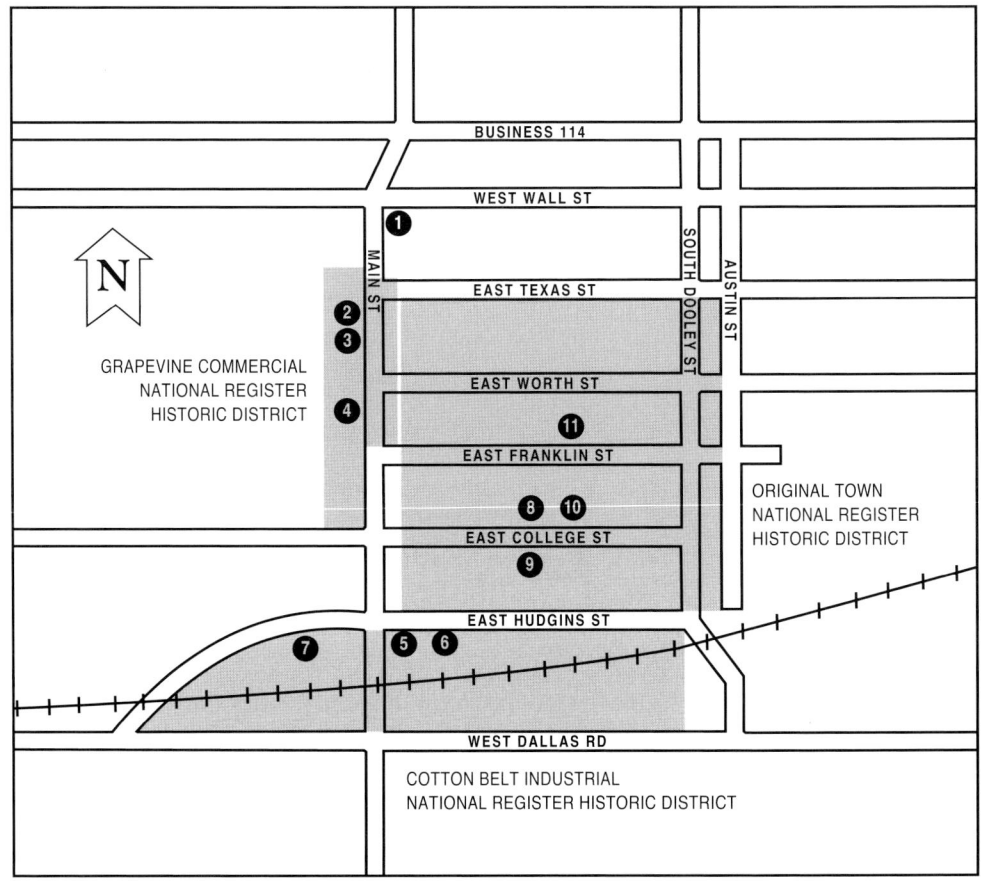

Grapevine

1. Torian Log Cabin

Grapevine Commercial National Register Historic District
2. Tarrant County State Bank
3. Grapevine Home Bank
4. Lucas Grocery

Cotton Belt Railroad Industrial National Register Historic District
5. Cotton Belt Depot
6. Cotton Belt Section House
7. B & D Mills

Original Town National Register Historic District
8. Stewart House
9. Dorris House
10. Wiggins House
11. Wall House

Northeast Tarrant County

Colleyville

People began to settle in the northeast Tarrant County area that is now Colleyville during the 1850s, locating in a number of small communities. Hilburn H. Colley, a physician, moved here during the 1880s. He practiced medicine in the region for forty years, and his name became associated first with one settlement and later with the general area. Incorporated in 1956, Colleyville has benefited from its proximity to Fort Worth, where many of its residents are employed, and to the Dallas-Fort Worth International Airport.

Bidault House, 1416 Glade Road, 1905-1911 (RTHL)

French native Anthelm Bidault, a farmer and wine maker, designed and built this concrete house using blocks made from molds that he ordered from Sears Roebuck & Company. His farm included renowned orchards, berry fields, and a vineyard. During World War I, French soldiers stationed at Camp Bowie, just west of Fort Worth, were entertained in the house. Bidault was not the first Frenchman to grow grapes for wine in this region. During the 1850s, the La Reunion Colony just west of Dallas also established vineyards, but the soil – which looked similar to that in the good wine regions of France – did not produce quality grapes. Bidault and his family returned to France in 1920. This house is not mapped in this book.

Grapevine

Named for the numerous wild grapevines that once grew in the region Grape Vine – or Grapevine as it was known after 1914 – was first settled during the late 1840s and early 1850s. Located approximately nineteen miles northeast of Fort Worth, the community functioned as a trading, transportation, and agricultural processing center for the region. The St. Louis, Arkansas, and Texas Railway, later named the St. Louis and Southwestern Railway, the "Cotton Belt Route," arrived in 1888, spurring development when farmers gained the ability to ship their products via rail. Always a small town with between eight hundred and twenty-eight hundred residents prior to 1960, Grapevine grew rapidly after the Dallas Fort Worth International Airport opened in 1974 at the southeastern edge of the city. Grapevine has worked to preserve its strong core of historic businesses and homes that give the center of town a pleasing historic ambiance and small-town feel.

1. Torian Log Cabin, 211 S. Main Street, c. 1845-1860 (RTHL)

This cabin originally stood beside a creek on Dove Road in the pioneer community of Dove. The land on which it stood was settled in 1845 by Francis Throop, a Peters colonist, and changed ownership several times. John R. Torian bought the property in 1886, and members of the Torian family lived here through the 1940s. The cabin was moved about four miles to Liberty Park in Grapevine in 1976 and reconstructed as a museum. It is a typical double-pen cabin consisting of two connecting rooms side by side, each with an outer door to the porch.

Grapevine Commercial National Register Historic District

The Grapevine Commercial Historic District is a collection of buildings that typify the main street of a small, circa 1900 agricultural community that, like many others in the region, experienced significant suburban growth in the latter half of the twentieth century, drawing business and commerce away to the town's fringes. The historic district contains one- and two-story commercial buildings constructed at the turn of the century and located along Main Street. The buildings comprise the most intact portion of Grapevine's historic mercantile center. Most of the buildings are built of red brick, and all have recessed storefront entries flanked by large plate glass shop windows topped by transoms.

2. Tarrant County State Bank Building, 332 S. Main Street, 1897, 1921 (RTHL)

Constructed in 1897, this building served as retail space until it was purchased and remodeled by the Tarrant County State Bank in 1921. It became the offices of the *Grapevine Sun* newspaper in 1947. The classic, small-scale banking-temple design features a central inset entry and a stepped-brick parapet. Inside, the wood-paneled bank interior is still intact.

3. Grapevine Home Bank, 404-406 S. Main Street, c. 1900

Grapevine Home Bank was a private bank, owned and managed by Robert "Bob" Morrow. He housed his banking operations here until 1933, when federal regulations were imposed. An insurance agency occupied the building between 1933 and 1968. Located on the corner of Main and Worth streets, the one-story, red brick structure has distinctive, almost fortress-like piers flanking the main entrance. Banks, particularly small-town banks, often signify their security and stability by means of the building's design.

4. Lucas Grocery, 412 S. Main Street, c. 1900; 1910

The bottom story of this small commercial building was built in 1900, and the second story added about 1910. The Lucas family operated a grocery and farm implements store on the first floor and ran a funeral home from the second floor. This building is probably the most distinguished example in an impressive row of four turn-of-the-century brick commercial buildings along the west side of Main Street. The exceptional detailing includes the stepped façade, decorative brickwork in the cornice, and the cast iron columns on the ground floor.

Cotton Belt Railroad Industrial National Register Historic District

The Cotton Belt Railroad Industrial Historic District contains properties associated with the development of the transportation and agricultural processing industries in Grapevine. Occupying tracts adjacent to the railroad right-of-way just south of the town's commercial district, the complex includes both turn-of-the-century buildings constructed for the Cotton Belt Railway and mid-twentieth-century utilitarian structures built to take advantage of easy access to the rail line.

5. *Cotton Belt Depot, 705 S. Main Street, 1901*

Replacing an earlier depot, this structure was constructed in 1901 using standard plans developed in Cotton Belt corporate offices for use throughout the system. The rectangular depot with weatherboard siding is located adjacent to the railroad tracks. It originally contained two freight rooms, two offices, a storage room, and two waiting rooms (one for African Americans and one for whites) separated by a seven-foot wall.

When the building was declared surplus by the railroad and threatened with demolition, the Grapevine Historical Society formed to acquire the depot and move it to Heritage Park. Eventually, the Grapevine Heritage Foundation was able to purchase the land on which the depot originally stood, move the building back to its original site, and restore it. Today the station houses the Grapevine Historical Museum and serves as a depot for the Grapevine Vintage Railroad that runs between Grapevine and the Fort Worth Stockyards.

6. *Cotton Belt Section House, 709 S. Main Street, 1888*

The Cotton Belt line built this section house in 1888 to house railroad workers. The two-story, L-plan house has weatherboard siding and is painted yellow and brown, the color scheme used for Cotton Belt buildings. Inside, the house had a living room, kitchen, dining room, and one bedroom downstairs, with two bedrooms on the second floor. Heat was provided by a wood-burning stove, often using old cross ties as fuel. Restored by the Grapevine Heritage Foundation, the house is now leased to the Grapevine Vintage Railroad for its office operations.

7. *Farmers & Merchants Milling Company/B & D Mills, Ira E. Woods Avenue at Church Street, 1902, 1936, c. 1949-1950*

Located on a site with direct railroad access, this facility has long been the major feature on Grapevine's skyline. From a three-story wooden building constructed in 1902 to mill flour and cornmeal, the complex has expanded over the years to include a grain elevator, a series of concrete

silos, two riveted steel plate storage tanks, and several corrugated metal utility buildings. B & D Mills bought the complex in 1936, converted it to a feed mill, and operated the facility until 1973. Despite a fire in 1995, the mill complex remains a good example of industrial facilities active during the first half of the twentieth century.

Original Town National Register Residential Historic District

The Original Town Residential Historic District encompasses Grapevine's most intact neighborhood of late-nineteenth- and early-twentieth-century residential properties. Located east of the town's historic commercial center, most of the houses are frame and brick dwellings erected between about 1890 and about 1950. Many of the most impressive homes are located along College Street.

8. Stewart House, 223 E. College Street, c. 1915

This handsome multi-colored brick house was built about 1915 for Clarence Stewart, a farmer and three-term member of the Texas Legislature. Stewart sold it to his brother Clarence in 1917, and it remained in the Stewart family through the 1970s. Sited on a corner lot, this Prairie-style house complements the Mary Lipscomb Wiggins house on the facing corner at 307 E. College Street. Although different from the Wiggins house in its use of materials and details, the Stewart house is its mirror in design.

9. Dorris House, 224 E. College Street, 1896

This handsome Queen Anne-style house, built in 1896 for physician Thomas Benton Dorris, is one of Grapevine's most striking residential structures. Frank and Charles Estill, local lumbermen and master builders, constructed several architecturally sophisticated residences here at the turn of the century, including the Dorris House. The home's impressive detailing includes fish-scale shingles, scroll-sawn brackets, and delicate window hoods. Dorris practiced medicine in Grapevine between 1885 and his death in 1918 and served as a railroad surgeon. His house is itself symbolic of the prosperity Grapevine enjoyed after the arrival of the railroad in 1888.

10. Wiggins House, 307 E. College Street, 1915-1916

Fort Worth architect Frank Singleton designed this fine example of a Prairie-style house for Mary Lipscomb Wiggins, an educator. It features many hallmarks of Prairie School design, including a low hipped roof, broad overhanging eaves, an expansive wraparound porch, and numerous banks of double-hung windows that combine to create a strong horizontal composition.

11. Wall House, 421 Smith Street, 1904

Fort Worth architects Sanguinet and Staats designed this Classical Revival house for community leader Benjamin R. Wall. Wall was the first

elected mayor of Grapevine, publisher of the *Grapevine Sun* newspaper, and founder of the Farmers & Merchants Milling Company as well as surveyor, realtor, and attorney. The curved, wraparound porch and the unusual roof dormer with curving shingled walls distinguish this handsome design.

Bedford

Bedford, located between Fort Worth and Grapevine in Northeast Tarrant County on State Highway 121, was first settled during the late 1840s. It did not begin to develop until the 1870s, when Weldon Bobo moved to the area from Tennessee and opened a gristmill and general store to serve nearby farmers. The town thrived during the late nineteenth century and had more residents than any other Tarrant County community except Fort Worth. After the Interurban, the Rock Island Railroad, and U. S. Highway 80 bypassed Bedford during the first decades of the twentieth century, the community's population shrank and was stable through the 1940s. Bedford incorporated in 1953, as post-World War II growth turned many small rural towns between Dallas and Fort Worth into suburban communities. The opening of nearby Dallas Fort Worth International Airport in 1974 encouraged an even larger growth spurt.

Bedford School, 2400 School Lane, 1914-1915 (NR & OTHM)
Built on the site of the old Bedford College founded in 1882, the Bedford School is one of the last surviving traces of the early Bedford community. It was built at a time when the town's population had shrunk

to about fifty people, the post office had closed, and truck farming and dairies were the primary forms of commerce. Grapevine builders Frank and Charles Estill erected the two-story brick building at a cost of $5,000. Open until 1969, the school functioned as a physical, social, educational, and cultural landmark in Bedford. The building suffered a disastrous fire in 1991 that galvanized community support to restore it. After almost two decades of use as a warehouse and vehicle repair facility for the school district, the building was restored in 1991 and currently serves as a community arts center. The Bedford School represents the period of development in Bedford when citizens regarded the school as the centerpiece of the rural, unincorporated community. The structure is not mapped in this book.

West Tarrant County

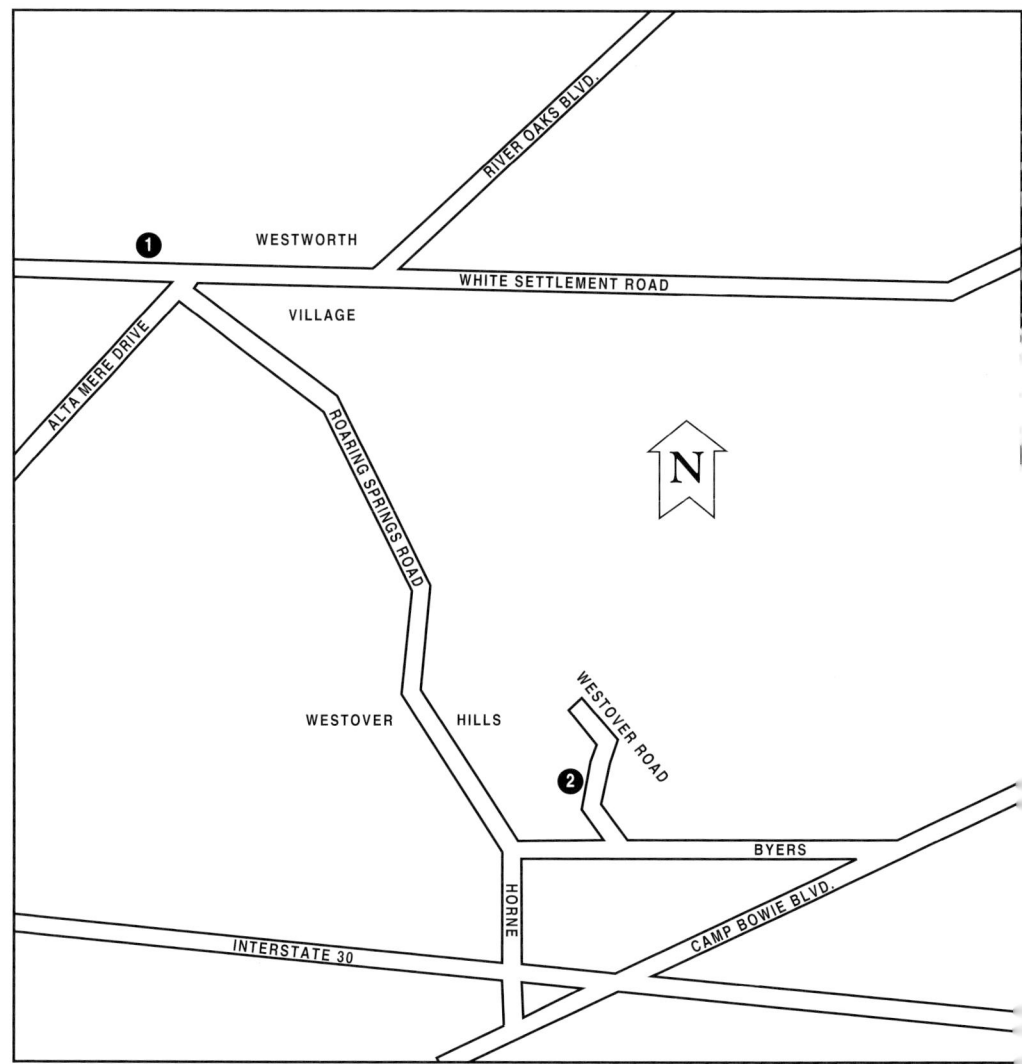

West Tarrant County

1. Buck Oaks Farm
2. Westover Manor

West Tarrant County

Westworth Village

Although there were scattered residences throughout the area that now comprises Westworth Village, the decision in 1941 to build what would become Carswell Air Force base was the impetus for incorporating this small western Tarrant County community. Westworth Village thrived through the early 1970s because many residents worked either at Carswell or at the nearby General Dynamics aircraft plant, now Lockheed-Martin, and the town enjoyed benefits resulting from the growth in the defense industry. Military downsizing following the war in Vietnam also affected growth in Westworth Village, leaving it a smaller, yet stable, community.

1. Buck Oaks Farm, 6312 White Settlement Road, 1932 (NR)

Typical of a number of country estates that once dotted the rural landscape in western Tarrant County, Buck Oaks Farm was built for Fort

Worth businessman Raymond E. Buck and his wife Katherine as their "dream house." Many of these estates have since fallen to suburban development. Buck purchased seventeen acres of land, including a portion of pioneer Elijah Farmer's farm, and hired local architect Earl T. Glasgow to design this Colonial Revival home built of rubble stone and clapboard. Sited on a gentle hill and angled to meet the contours of the site, the house features five large rock-and-brick fireplaces, rustic beams, and custom-crafted wrought iron-and-wood light fix-  tures. The military facility that became Carswell Air Force Base was built nearby in 1942, and during the early 1950s Buck sold both the house and grounds to the government for use as officer housing. After Carswell became the Naval Air Station/Joint Reserve Base, Buck Oaks Farm was transferred to a nonprofit organization created to redevelop unneeded portions of the base.

Westover Hills

Westover Hills is an exclusive residential enclave located about four-and-one-half miles west of Fort Worth's central business district. Although a separately incorporated town, it is completely surrounded by Fort Worth. Westover Hills was organized in 1923 by the Fort Worth Extension Company and platted in 1928 as a deed-restricted community that required masonry construction, a minimum cost, and company approval of plans for any home built in the development. Few homes were built during the 1920s, and the hilly terrain quickly acquired the name "Leftover Hills." Byrne & Luther, Inc., a contracting firm, began to build homes in Westover Hills during the 1930s using plans drawn by local architects, a move that intensified the pace of development. The community incorporated in 1937 to avoid annexation by Fort Worth, even though the larger city provided water to Westover Hills. Fort Worth cut off the new town's water supply, beginning a series of lawsuits and negotiations over water service and rates that continued for many years.

2. Westover Manor, 8 Westover Road, 1930 (NR)

Westover Manor was built as the *Fort Worth Star-Telegram's* 1930 "Home Beautiful," part of a publicity program to help market the development. Designed by architect Victor Marr Curtis, the large Norman-Tudor Period Revival home was constructed by Byrne & Luther, Inc. At the time, it was the largest home in Westover Hills and served as an example of the type of mansion the developers wanted to see built here. Open to the public for tours during the summer of 1930, the home sold that September for $50,000 to oilman John E. Farrell, one of the discoverers of the extremely profitable oil fields in East Texas. Farrell was also elected the first mayor of Westover Hills after the town was incorporated, and he lived here until his death in 1946.

Cemeteries

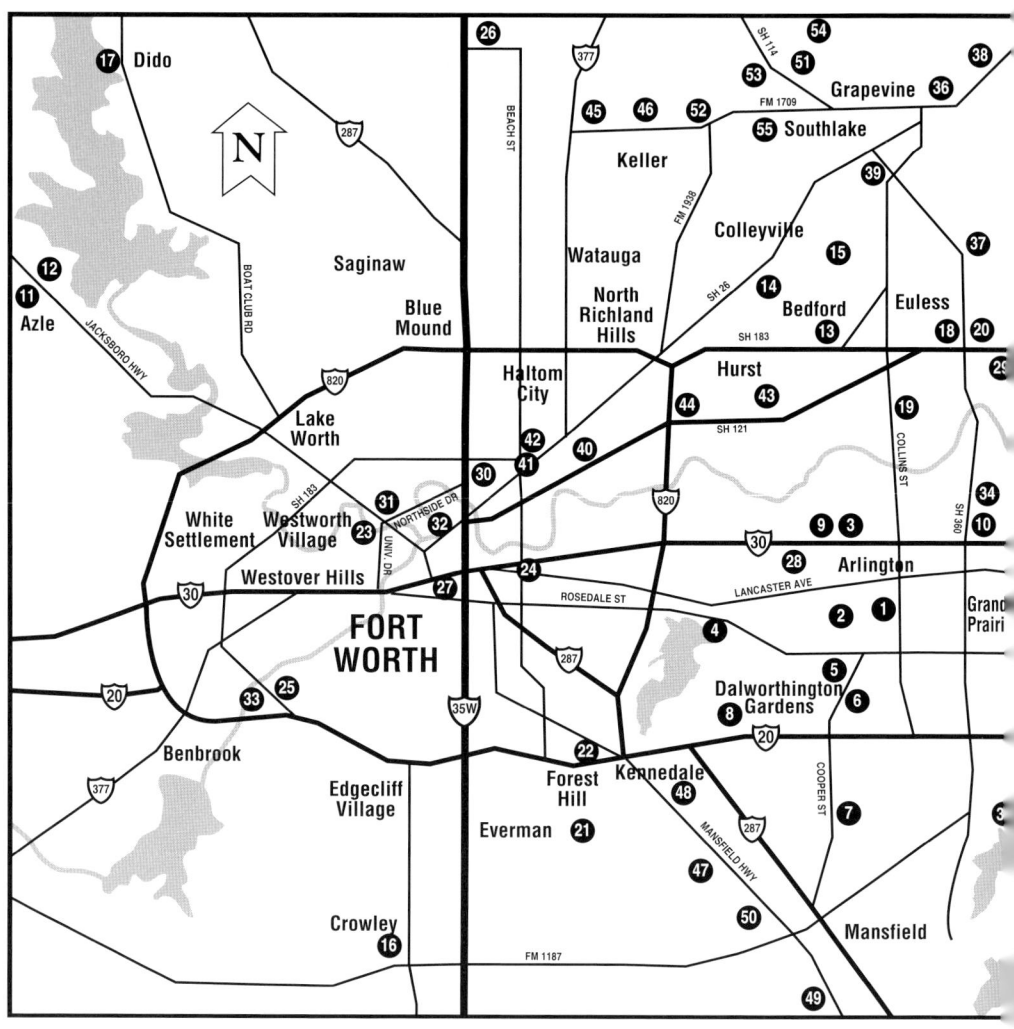

Cemeteries

All have Official Texas Historical Markers, unless otherwise indicated.

Arlington
1. Arlington Cemetery
2. Berachah Home and Cemetery
3. Gibbins Cemetery
4. Handley Cemetery
5. Middleton Tate Johnson Plantation Cemetery
6. Johnson Station Cemetery
7. Rehoboth Cemetery
8. Tate Cemetery
9. Tomlin Cemetery
10. P. A. Watson Cemetery

Azle
11. Ash Creek Cemetery
12. Smith-Frazier Cemetery

Bedford
13. Bedford Cemetery

Colleyville
14. Riley Cemetery
15. Witten Cemetery

Crowley
16. Crowley Cemetery

Dido
17. Dido Cemetery

Euless
18. Bear Creek Cemetery
19. Calloway Cemetery
20. Alexander Dobkins Family Cemetery

Everman
21. Everman Cemetery

Forest Hill
22. Forest Hill Cemetery

Fort Worth
23. Ahavath Sholom Hebrew Cemetery
24. Ayres Cemetery
25. Burke Cemetery
26. Chapel Cemetery
27. Emanuel Hebrew Rest Cemetery
28. Harrison Cemetery
29. Hitch Cemetery
30. Mount Olivet Cemetery
31. Oakwood Cemetery and Chapel
32. Pioneers Rest Cemetery
33. Willburn Cemetery

Grand Prairie
34. Ford Cemetery
35. Wilson Cemetery

Grapevine
36. Grapevine Cemetery
37. Minter's Chapel Cemetery
38. Morgan Hood Survey Pioneer Cemetery
39. Parker Memorial Cemetery

Haltom City
40. Birdville Cemetery
41. Harper's Rest Cemetery
42. New Trinity Cemetery

Hurst
43. Arwine Cemetery
44. Parker Cemetery

Keller
45. Bourland Cemetery
46. Mount Gilead Cemetery

Kennedale
47. Hudson Cemetery
48. Rodgers Cemetery

Mansfield
49. Cumberland Presbyterian Cemetery
50. Gibson Cemetery

Southlake
51. Absalom H. Chivers Cemetery
52. Thomas Easter Cemetery
53. Hood Cemetery
54. Lonesome Dove Baptist Church and Cemetery
55. White's Chapel Cemetery

Arlington

1. Arlington Cemetery, 801 Mary Street

Encompassing more than ten acres of land, Arlington Cemetery includes within its borders several small historic graveyards, including the William W. McNatt Cemetery, the Masonic Cemetery, and the Old City Cemetery. McNatt, who brought his family here from Arkansas in 1872, was a retail merchant and farmer. He sold some of his property to the Arlington Cemetery Society in 1899. Another group, the Arlington Cemetery Association, was chartered in 1923 and maintained the graveyard for many years until the City of Arlington assumed ownership and maintenance. The oldest documented burial here is that of one-year-old Mattie Luna Cooper, who died in 1875. Numerous early Arlington settlers also are buried here, as are veterans of conflicts from the Civil War to World War II. Local officials interred in the graveyard include seven former postmasters and ten former mayors.

2. Berachah Home and Cemetery, Mitchell Street (in Doug Russell Park near the University of Texas at Arlington)

Reverend James T. Upchurch organized the Berachah Rescue Society, an anti-prostitution organization, in Waco in 1894. Nine years later he opened the Berachah Industrial Home in Arlington, providing work for former prostitutes and other wayward young women as well as residential facilities for them and their children. At one time the complex consisted of ten buildings including a print shop that produced the *Purity Journal,* a magazine that exposed the evils of prostitution and told of Upchurch's success in rehabilitating the young women who came to live at the home. The cemetery, which contains more than eighty graves, was first used in 1904 for the burial of Eunice Williams, one of the residents. The home closed in 1935, but the site was used until 1942 as an orphanage run by Upchurch's daughter Allie Mae and her husband Frank Wiese.

3. Gibbins Cemetery and Homestead Site, 2200 N. Davis Drive

James Gibbins came to Texas from Arkansas in 1857 and bought land near present-day Arlington in 1863. He deeded part of this land to his son, Thomas, who used this family cemetery for the burial of his first wife, Amanda, who died in 1877. Martha H. Gibbins, Thomas Gibbins' second wife, maintained the land for three decades after the 1924 death of her husband. The Gibbins family contributed land for a public school and much of the land for River Legacy Parks.

4. Handley Cemetery, off Spur 303 on Lake Arlington Dam Road (There is no road access to this cemetery.)

This burial ground originally served the pioneer settlers of the Handley community. The earliest marked grave is that of Jane E. Thomas, who died in 1878. A church building, constructed on adjacent land in 1882, was located here for forty-eight years. Civil War veteran Major James M. Handley, who died in 1906 and for whom the town of Handley was named, was first buried here but later re-interred in nearby Rose Hill Cemetery. The last burial here occurred in 1967.

5. Middleton Tate Johnson Plantation Cemetery and Park, 621 West Arkansas Lane

This site was once part of the extensive land holdings of Colonel Middleton Tate Johnson, who is buried in the cemetery. Johnson, an Alabama native and friend of Andrew Jackson and Sam Houston, served in both the Alabama and Texas legislatures. Johnson County to the south was named for him in 1854 after his unsuccessful bid for the governorship. Several log structures from pioneer communities that predate Arlington have been moved to this park, including two log cabins, an early one-room school house, and a barn. Two area Interurban stations and the well bowl from the mineral water well in the center of Arlington were also relocated to the park.

6. Johnson Station Cemetery, 1111 W. Mayfield Road

Now part of Arlington, this area was established in the 1840s as a ranger station and trading post known as Johnson Station. Located in a large two-story house that no longer stands, the station also served as a stop on the Overland Stage route. The oldest marked grave in the cemetery belongs to Elizabeth Robinson who died in 1863, but there may be unmarked graves from an earlier time period.

7. Rehoboth Cemetery, Corner of T. O. Harris Road and S. Cooper Street

The Rehoboth Cemetery was established in 1871 with the burial of infant Mary Miller. The cemetery served the community of Sublett, named after John Sublett, which consisted of a school, post office, and church. The one-room schoolhouse, also used by the Rehoboth Baptist Church, once stood next to the cemetery. The two-and-one-half acre site contains more than five hundred graves, although many of the headstones are illegible.

8. Tate Cemetery, 4200 block of Pleasant Ridge Road

E. C. Tate moved to Texas from Georgia and settled in southeast Tarrant County about 1872. He established the Tate Springs community and, in 1882, helped organize the Tate Springs Church. Tate was buried at this site in 1885, and by 1894 three of his children had also been buried in this family cemetery. Also in 1894, Tate's son Robert designated the acre of land containing the family burials as a community cemetery. Robert Tate's own grave is unmarked, as are some thirty-five other burials. Most graves belong to members of the Tate family and residents of Tate Springs.

9. Tomlin Cemetery, Tomlin Lane (west from N. Davis Drive)

This cemetery was first used in the 1870s by the Wilkinson family, and their graves are marked by clusters of rocks. The oldest dated gravestone is that of Soloman Tomlin, a horseman and farmer who brought his family to Texas in the 1860s and who died in 1884. His son James Tives "Buck" Tomlin, a noted breeder of fine racing horses, bought the cemetery property in 1888. It has since served as a burial ground for descendants of the Tomlin Family.

10. P. A. Watson Cemetery, 1024 N. Watson Road (SH 360)

Mrs. Micajah Goodwin was buried here in 1846 in a coffin made from the bed of the family wagon. Brush was burned atop her grave to hide it from the Indians. There were other graves here when Patrick Alfred Watson, a civic-minded settler, bought the land in 1852 and set aside a one-acre cemetery. Watson also gave land for the Watson community's first school and church in 1870. In 1956 the Dallas-Fort Worth Turnpike was routed around the cemetery. The Watson cabin, now in the Johnson Plantation Cemetery and Park, was originally located nearby.

Azle

11. Ash Creek Cemetery, 310 S. Stewart Street

The oldest known graves in this community burial ground are those of Dave Morrison and W. P. Gregg, both of whom died in 1874. Dr. James Azle Steward, for whom Azle is named, and John Giles Reynolds, an early grist mill operator, each donated an acre of land to establish the cemetery. Both men are also buried here. The Azle Cemetery Association was organized in 1922 to care for the site and to keep burial records. The cemetery has been enlarged over the years and contains more than two thousand graves.

12. Smith-Frazier Cemetery, 300 block S. Ash Avenue

Fort Worth businessman and philanthropist J. J. Jarvis bought land here in 1871 and built a home on the property during the early 1880s. In 1886, Jarvis gave a section of his land to Charles Young and Allen Prince for use as a burial ground for Azle's African-American residents. There were already several graves here at that time. The cemetery was later inherited by descendants of the pioneer Smith and Frazier families and is still in use.

Bedford

13. Bedford Cemetery, 2401 Bedford Road

Pioneers probably began using this graveyard during the 1860s. The earliest marked grave is that of Bettie W. Bobo, a child who died in 1871. In 1877 Milton Moore deeded a five-acre tract, including this cemetery, to New Hope Church of Christ. The Bedford Church Old Settlers Reunion met here annually for over fifty years. William Letchworth Hurst, for whom the nearby town of Hurst is named, is buried here as are many pioneer Bedford residents, a number of whom lie in unmarked graves. The Bedford Cemetery Association acquired the site in 1975.

Colleyville

14. Riley Cemetery, 3700 block of Brown Trail Drive at Morning Glory Lane

Jonathan Riley, who brought his family to this area from Kentucky, received this land grant in 1863. In 1877, horse thief John Alison Goldsmith was shot and killed while trying to escape from sheriff's deputies. Local legend says that Riley gave permission for his burial here. In 1883, Thomas Riley and William Autry set aside this one-acre tract for a graveyard. By then, family and neighbors had also used the cemetery. Riley's descendants left the area before 1890, but the cemetery was used until near the turn of the century. There was one new interment during the 1930s. Many graves are now designated only with sandstones, and the rest are unmarked.

15. Witten Cemetery, Jackson Court (cul-de-sac off 4700 block of Jackson Road)

Samuel Cecil Holiday Witten, a successful landowner, justice of the peace, and Tarrant County surveyor, came to Texas in 1854. He first used this burial site in 1857 for the interment of his son, William Cecil. His son-in-law, Ryan Harrington, a frontiersman who participated in the 1849 California gold rush, is also buried here. Although Witten and his family moved to Corpus Christi in 1890, the cemetery remained in use by family members for a number of years thereafter.

Crowley

16. Crowley Cemetery, 300 N. Hampton Road

Settlers who moved into the Deer Creek area in the late 1840s first used this cemetery. The earliest grave is that of Thomas D. Stephenson, an eight-year-old boy who died in 1857. The property was deeded for use as a public burial site in 1879 by Sarah J. "Sallie" Dunn. Originally known as Deer Creek Cemetery, the name of the cemetery was changed in the 1880s soon after the town of Crowley was organized.

Dido

17. Dido Cemetery, 5570 Dido-Hicks Road at Morris-Dido-Newark Road.

Amanda Thurmond, the infant granddaughter of Dave Thurmond, was the first person buried in this cemetery in 1879. In 1887, Dempsy S. Holt, the landowner, donated three acres of land to the Dido community for a school, church, and cemetery. Dr. Isaac L. Van Zandt, a pioneer physician and Confederate veteran, gave additional land in 1894. Dido, once a thriving community with a post office and several stores, was named for the mythological queen of Carthage. The village declined after the railroad bypassed it in the 1890s, but several families still live in Dido, and the cemetery is still active. There are about one thousand graves, including that of singer-songwriter Townes Van Zandt whose ashes were placed in the Van Zandt family plot.

Euless

18. Bear Creek Cemetery, 1400 block of Minters Chapel Road

This cemetery was developed adjacent to the site of the Bear Creek Missionary Baptist Church. The earliest marked grave is that of Hiram Jackson Farris, an infant who died in 1858. Isham Crowley, who came to Texas as a member of Peters Colony, gave the burial ground to church trustees in 1876. Although the congregation later moved to Dallas County and was renamed Western Heights Missionary Baptist Church, Bear Creek Cemetery is still in use.

19. Calloway Cemetery, 12600 Calloway Cemetery Road (near Euless in unincorporated Tarrant County)

The earliest marked graves here are those of two brothers, Richard H. and Joseph W. Calloway, who owned this land in the 1860s. Richard's widow Catherine deeded one-and-one-half acres here for use as a public burial ground in 1886. Members of the Calloway family and several of their neighbors are buried here. The wooden tabernacle was constructed in 1908, and family members maintained the grounds until 1971 when a perpetual care fund was set up.

20. Alexander Dobkins Family Cemetery, 1000 block of Minters Chapel Road

Alexander Dobkins and his wife, Mary, migrated to Texas from Tennessee in 1852. Ordained as a minister in nearby Bear Creek Missionary Baptist Church, Dobkins also served as a postmaster for Estill's Station during the Civil War. Dobkins died in 1869, and his grave is the earliest marked one in this cemetery, which was originally part of his two-hundred-acre farm. There are seven burials in this graveyard, all members of the Dobkins family. The cemetery is located on land owned by Dallas-Fort Worth International Airport and is closed to all except family members for security reasons.

Everman

21. Everman Cemetery, 800 E. Enon Street

The first settlement in this area, called Enon, began about 1847. After the railroad was built in 1903, townspeople relocated to be near the rail line and renamed their community Everman for John W. Everman, a railroad engineer. R. E. Morris, whose wife Rosa was interred on the family farm, established the Everman Cemetery in 1882. Called the Morris Graveyard for many years, the cemetery was eventually renamed to reflect its use as a community burial ground.

Forest Hill

22. Forest Hill Cemetery, 5713 Forest Hill Drive

One of the oldest burial grounds in southeast Tarrant County, this cemetery was used for many years before records were kept. Pioneer settlers Press and Jane Farmer, who lived in the area before the U. S. Army established the military post called Fort Worth in 1849, are buried here. Press Farmer served as the fort's sutler or storekeeper. Few headstones are visible because most graves were unmarked or marked only with field-stones that have since disappeared. The cemetery is full, however.

Fort Worth

23. Ahavath Sholom Hebrew Cemetery, 415 N. University Drive

Congregation Ahavath Sholom, the first Jewish congregation in Fort Worth, was established in 1892 and purchased a six-acre tract from the Greenwood Cemetery Association at this location in 1909. The first person buried here was Charles Hurwitz, who died in 1910. The cemetery was enlarged in 1929. Among the graves are those of three soldiers who were killed during World War II and are buried side by side in the north section of the cemetery. A large monument memorializing the millions of Jewish victims killed during World War II was erected by families of those who died during the Holocaust. The Kornbleet Chapel, which contains seating for one hundred persons, was dedicated in 1988. It is used for funeral services as well as other religious services. The cemetery is still active.

24. Ayres Cemetery, 2500 block of Scott Street

Benjamin Patton Ayres and his wife, Emily, bought a 320-acre farm on this hillside in 1861 and set aside two acres as a family cemetery. Ayres served as the second Tarrant County Clerk when the county seat was located in Birdville and helped organize Fort Worth's First Christian Church. He was the first person buried here in 1862. An unknown number of unmarked graves, which lie outside the Ayres family plot, include victims of spring fevers and Trinity River floods. The Ayres family plot was reserved when descendants sold the property, and the fenced graveyard is now surrounded by a motel parking lot.

25. Burke Cemetery, 3500 Bryant Irvin Road

Mary Overton Burke, the widow of Evan H. Burke, moved to this area in 1851 with her children and widowed mother. The family settled on land previously chosen by her husband. Mrs. Burke died in 1867 and was the first person buried in this graveyard, followed two days later by her mother. In 1900 this one-half acre of land was deeded as a family burial ground. Burke Cemetery contains over one hundred graves, including those of members of the Magers, Overton, and Edwards families. It is located at the south end of the Lockheed-Martin Recreation Area.

26. Chapel Cemetery, 14200 block of Old Denton Road (near Denton County line in unincorporated Tarrant County)

According to family tradition, this cemetery began with the burial of Eliny Raibourn in 1856 and the subsequent donation of land for cemetery purposes by her brother-in-law, John Fanning. Subsequently, the site became known as the Fanning burying grounds. A one-room school located one mile to the south was the only community facility in this area until a chapel was built next to the cemetery. Sweet Chapel Methodist Church purchased both the chapel and cemetery in 1893, and the burying ground became known as the Sweet Chapel Cemetery. By 1938, the chapel had been demolished and the cemetery came to be called simply, Chapel Cemetery. Burials continued on an informal basis for many years. Mount Olivet Cemetery Association acquired this private cemetery in 1985 and operates it, with burial rights granted only to relatives of those already interred there.

27. Emanuel Hebrew Rest Cemetery, 1414 S. Main Street

John Peter Smith donated land here in 1879 for use as the first cemetery for the city's Jewish residents. The earliest marked grave is that of Leah Kaiser, a child who died in 1879. First maintained by the Emanuel Hebrew Association, the cemetery is now managed by the Beth-El Congregation. Members of the Jewish faith were among early settlers in Fort Worth. Ahavath Shalom, a conservative congregation, was organized in 1892 followed by Beth-El, a reform congregation, in 1902. Many prominent Fort Worth Jewish professional, business, and civic leaders are buried here among the three hundred graves.

28. Harrison Cemetery, 8550 Meadowbrook Drive

This one-acre cemetery originally belonged to pioneer D. C. Harrison. The earliest known grave is that of Mary E. Harrison, who died in 1871. R. A. Randol operated Randol Mill, a grain mill, circular saw, and cotton gin nearby between 1876 and 1922. He purchased the land in 1895 and recorded it as a cemetery in the deed records. His first wife, mother-in-law, and brother are buried here among the approximately sixty graves. Many of the headstones have disappeared, so it is difficult to recognize this piece of land as a cemetery.

29. Hitch Cemetery, at dead end of Kingsport Road

This cemetery was once part of a large farm owned by Kentucky native William Henry Hitch, who brought his family here from Tennessee in 1855. He buried his son, Haden, here in 1858, the first burial in the cemetery. Hitch had encouraged several other Kentucky families to move to Texas with him, and a number of those settlers are also buried here.

30. Mount Olivet Cemetery, 2205 N. Sylvania Avenue

Originally part of Charles B. Daggett's land, this 130-acre cemetery was dedicated in 1907 by Flavius G. McPeak and was the first perpetual care cemetery in the area. Its forty-seven thousand burials include 594 victims of the 1918 flu epidemic, the McPeaks and members of their families, as well as many early Tarrant County settlers. The oldest marked grave is that of Zenas Ewin Kerr who was buried here in 1907. McPeak patterned the landscaped grounds after the Mount Olivet Cemetery in Nashville, Tennessee. The cemetery contains a number of sculptures including a bas-relief of Da Vinci's painting, "The Lord's Supper," a statue depicting Christ's crucifixion surrounded by the graves of priests and nuns, and two monuments honoring veterans. Special Memorial Day observances are held here each year to honor deceased war veterans.

31. Oakwood Cemetery and Chapel, 701 Grand Avenue (RTHL)

In 1879, John Peter Smith, one of the city's first settlers and most prominent civic leaders, gave twenty acres to the city for this cemetery on a bluff overlooking downtown Fort Worth. It was eventually enlarged to cover one hundred acres. There are actually three cemeteries – Oakwood, Calvary for Catholics, and Trinity for African Americans – within these boundaries. The cemetery contains a number of specialized sites including Solders' Row, established in 1903 for the burial of Confederate veterans, as well as plots used by a bricklayers' union, bartenders, fraternal lodges, and paupers. A life-sized Confederate soldier, made of Italian marble, was erected by the United Daughters of the Confederacy in a plot reserved for Confederate soldiers and their wives. The plot reserved for Union soldiers similarly has a bronze marker.

Many prominent citizens are buried in Oakwood Cemetery, including John Peter Smith, the original donor of the land. Other well-known people buried here include rancher and oilman Samuel Burk Burnett, Euday Louis Bowman who composed the "12th Street Rag," cattleman W. T. Waggoner, saloon owner Luke Short, financier Winfield Scott, and African-American banker and political leader William Madison McDonald.

Architects Marion L. Waller and E. Stanley Field designed Oakwood Chapel. The charming Gothic Revival structure was built in 1912 with funds raised by the sale of cemetery plots. A series of heavy vaults in the lower level were formerly used for the storage of bodies brought from out of town. In the early days, a trap door was used to lower caskets to the waiting horse-drawn hearses. In 1974, the Fort Worth Chapter of Women in Construction restored the chapel as a special project. The cemetery is still active.

32. Pioneers Rest Cemetery, 626 Samuels Avenue

When two of the children of Major Ripley Arnold, commander of the troops at Fort Worth, died during the summer of 1850, his good friend Dr. Adolphus Gouhenant allowed the children to be buried on his land. Baldwin L. Samuel gave three more acres in 1871, and many years later a cemetery association was formed. Major Ripley Arnold, General Edward H. Tarrant – the man for whom Tarrant County is named, civic leader Ephraim M. Daggett, pioneer physician Carroll M. Peak, and seventy-five Civil War veterans are all buried at Pioneers Rest.

33. Willburn Cemetery, 3720 Streamwood Road

Many of the individuals buried in this pioneer cemetery are descendants of Edward and Nancy Willburn who moved to Texas from Missouri in 1843 as members of the Peters Colony and to southwestern Tarrant County in 1854. Edward Willburn built the first school in this area in 1857. The "Old Rawhide" school replaced it in 1872 and, after that building burned in 1879, Willburn's daughter, Marinda Willburn Snyder, donated land for another school. The school and the area around it was then known as Marinda, but the community was later renamed Benbrook in honor of James M. Benbrook. The earliest marked grave in the Willburn Cemetery is for the infant child of William and Cassandra Willburn, who died in 1867. Several other Willburn family members are also buried in this cemetery, which is located behind a high fence in the Ridglea Country Club Estates neighborhood.

Grand Prairie

34. Ford Cemetery, 602 Fountain Parkway (north of parking lot)

Pinkney Harold Ford and his family migrated from Kentucky to Texas in 1855 and settled in the area of Grand Prairie then known as the Watson community. A Civil War veteran and farmer, Ford purchased this property in 1879 from John J. Goodwin and designated it as a community burial ground. The earliest marked grave is that of Maria Trayler who died in 1858. Industrial development now surrounds the cemetery.

35. Wilson Cemetery, Lake Ridge Parkway (across from entrance to Lynn Creek Park at Joe Pool Lake)

This pioneer cemetery dates to 1872, when Charles N. Wilson buried his wife and infant child here. Both mother and daughter died as a result of complications during childbirth. James W. and Mattie C. Bowlin also buried their son here in an unmarked grave at a later date. The Wilson Cemetery contains only these three graves, but it is an important reminder of the harsh reality of life in nineteenth-century Tarrant County.

Grapevine

36. Grapevine Cemetery, North Dooley Street and Wildwood Lane

In 1878, brothers Samuel D. and Allen B. Coble sold four-and-one-half acres of their land here for use as a public cemetery. The earliest grave

is that of Louisa C. Guiry who died in 1860 at the age of twenty-two. Pioneer settlers buried here include Barton H. Starr, the first mayor of Grapevine, and James Tracy Morehead, the second judge of Tarrant County. The cemetery was enlarged in 1925 and is still in use.

37. Minter's Chapel Cemetery, W. Airfield Drive (one quarter mile north of the Glade Road intersection)

Lay Minister Green W. Minter organized Minter's Chapel Methodist Church in 1854. His son-in-law, James Cate, set aside slightly over four acres for a church and a burial ground. The earliest grave is that of A. M. Newton who died in 1857. In 1882, the original log meeting house was replaced by a frame structure. Dallas-Fort Worth Airport acquired the land in 1967 as part of the buffer zone surrounding the runways. The church was relocated to Grapevine, but the cemetery remains on the west side of the airport.

38. Morgan Hood Survey Pioneer Cemetery, State Highway 2, (one quarter mile southwest of Bethel Road)

Originally part of the Morgan Hood Survey, this small cemetery has been abandoned for over a century. Its one visible grave is marked by pieces of a sandstone burial cairn. Although no written records remain, the graves may be those of members of the Peters Colony who settled in this area in 1844.

39. Parker Memorial Cemetery, State Highway121 and Hall-Johnson Road (northwest corner, one block north of Hall-Johnson Road)

The first person buried here is thought to be Christina Driskill, mother-in-law of Isaac Green Parker, who owned the land. She died in 1862. In 1881, Parker's widow, Molly, deeded the land for a public burial ground for the Pleasant Glade community. Pleasant Glade, located approximately ten miles northeast of Fort Worth, had a church and a school. A tabernacle was erected on the cemetery grounds in 1928 and used first for funeral services and later for meetings of the cemetery association. Formerly known as Clements Cemetery, it was renamed in 1937. Both railroads and highways bypassed Pleasant Glade, and the cemetery is the only remnant of the community.

Haltom City

40. Birdville Cemetery, 6100 Cemetery Road

The oldest marked grave here belongs to Wiley Wilda Potts, who died in 1852. The one-acre tract, then part of the George Akers land grant, was legally set aside for burial purposes before 1860. More land was later donated, and by 1910 the site included over three-and-one-quarter acres. It now covers seven acres. The Birdville Cemetery Association, which cares for the grounds, was organized under a fifty-year charter in 1917 and re-chartered in 1967. Birdville developed from Bird's Fort, the first settlement in the county. It was established in 1841 and named for Captain Jonathan Bird. Birdville was a functioning settlement by 1848, and its earliest residents were farmers and cattle ranchers. It was selected by the state legislature as the county seat when Tarrant County was established in 1849 but lost the designation by seven votes to Fort Worth in a November 1856 election. It is now a part of Haltom City. The cemetery contains over five hundred graves, and several families have four generations buried here in the same family plot. The cemetery is still used today.

Judge Benjamin Franklin Barkley is one of the more interesting pioneers buried here. An opponent of slavery, Barkley emancipated the slaves on his Kentucky farm in 1855 and settled in Birdville with his family. A physician, lawyer, charter member of the Fort Worth Masonic Lodge, and Republican leader, Barkley spoke out against slavery and secession. Admired for donating land for Birdville's first school, participating in Indian campaigns, and supporting Birdville as the county seat, he nonetheless stirred anger and barely escaped death several times because of his strong pro-Union stand.

During the war, Barkley treated wounded Confederate soldiers and aided their families. At this time, he served as local postmaster, but during Reconstruction, he headed the County Registration Board, which denied the vote to former Confederate supporters. Appointed county judge in 1867, he used federal troops to maintain order. With great courage, he conducted a hearing on violent Ku Klux Klan activities. Barkley was defeated when Democrats won all county offices in 1873, but he remained active in law and medicine until his death. He is buried on land that he donated for the cemetery.

41. Harper's Rest Cemetery, 1804 Layton Avenue

Henry Jackson Harper and his family moved to this area from Tennessee in 1894. This cemetery was begun when the child of a family traveling through the area died and was buried in grove of trees on the Harper farm. Harper's grandson, Henry Mayton, was the first family member interred here in 1898. Other family burials include those of Harper children and grandchildren. Harper's wife Mary Jane died in 1922. He was buried next to her in 1928, and his is the last known burial in Harper's Rest Cemetery.

42. New Trinity Cemetery, 4001 NE 28th Street

When the Reverend Greene Fretwell, a former slave, died in 1886, there was no African-American cemetery in this part of Tarrant County. With donations collected by his widow, Frances, the trustees of Trinity Chapel Methodist Church bought two acres in 1889 for a church and burial ground. Worship services were held under a brush arbor until a frame church was built. By the 1920s, burials began on adjacent land, known as New Trinity Cemetery. Additional property was designated in 1931 as People's Burial Park. Today all three sites are referred to as New Trinity Cemetery.

Hurst

43. Arwine Cemetery, 700 block of Arwine Court

Daniel Arwine, raised in Indiana, began farming in Texas after the Civil War. A deputy U. S. marshal, he deeded six acres for a school, church, and cemetery in 1879. The first burial here was his daughter, Katy, who died in 1879. The grave of his uncle, Enoch Sexton who died in 1890, has the oldest gravestone in the cemetery. Arwine, his wife, and parents are among those buried in the 279 marked graves. His descendants and local Boy Scouts maintained the cemetery until the Arwine Cemetery Association was formed in 1975.

44. Parker Cemetery, 1300 block of Cardinal Road

Isaac Duke Parker, who donated land for this cemetery in 1901, was the son of Isaac Parker, the politician for whom Parker County is named and the uncle of Cynthia Ann Parker, the famous Comanche captive. During the Civil War, Isaac Duke Parker served as Tarrant County Commissioner before enlisting in the Confederate Army. He assumed ownership and operation of the Isaac Parker cabin and cemetery about 1867. Shortly before his death, Parker donated this cemetery property and designated the eastern half, which contains more than thirty graves, as a public burial ground. Like his father, Isaac Duke Parker served in the Texas Legislature. The Parker cabin currently stands in Log Cabin Village in Fort Worth.

Keller

45. Bourland Cemetery, Bourland Road, south of Bancroft Road

Aurelius Delphus Bourland, a Civil War veteran from North Carolina, bought land here in 1873. A farmer and Baptist preacher, he used this site as a private cemetery for his family. The earliest marked grave belongs to his infant grandson, A. Delphus White, who died in 1886. Bourland sold the site in 1899 for use as a public cemetery by the community of Keller. The red sandstone gateway was constructed by the Works Progress Administration in 1935. The cemetery is still use.

46. Mount Gilead Cemetery, Bancroft Road at Ottinger Road

This burial ground originally served the Peters Colony, a settlement of related families who came from Missouri in the late 1840s. Colony leader, Permelia Allen, who died in 1866, is buried here in an unmarked grave. Her sons-in-law, Daniel Bancroft and Iraneous Neace, first owned the site. The earliest marked grave is that of William Joyce, who died in 1854. Several of the grave markers are cairns, or mounds of stone, which are representative of traditional burial customs used in the South during the eighteenth and nineteenth centuries.

Kennedale

47. Hudson Cemetery, Hudson Cemetery Road, one-quarter mile west of Eden Road, (unincorporated Tarrant County, near Kennedale)

When Ary Mae and Arra Bell Hudson both died of measles in 1878, their parents buried them on the family land. Arra Bell, who died on a trip to Montague County, was first buried there and later brought back to the Hudson farm. In 1892, the Hudsons deeded three acres of land to the Hudson Cemetery trustees for use by the surrounding community. Most of the more than five hundred burials date from the early twentieth century, but the cemetery is still in use.

48. Rodgers Cemetery, Shady Oaks Drive and Kennedale-Little School Road

Thomas and Mary Rodgers moved to Texas from Kansas during the late 1850s. A successful farmer and stock raiser, Rodgers also served in the Confederate Army during the Civil War. By the time of his death, he was one of Kennedale's leading landowners. Most of the people buried here are members of the Rodgers family, but the earliest marked grave is that of L. G. Patterson, the son of Rodgers' neighbors, who died in 1884.

Mansfield

49. Cumberland Presbyterian Cemetery, Burl Ray Street (one tenth of a mile west of Second Avenue South)

This site was first used as a burial ground shortly after the Civil War, and the earliest legible gravestone is that of Julia Alice Boisseau Man who died in 1868. She was the wife of Ralph S. Man, co-founder of Mansfield. Their home still stands in Mansfield. Other graves hold Civil War veterans and victims of the 1918-1919 influenza epidemic. The cemetery was deeded to the Mansfield congregation of the Cumberland Presbyterian Church in 1874.

50. Gibson Cemetery, 7420 Gibson Cemetery Road (unincorporated Tarrant County, near Mansfield)

Garrett and James Gibson and their families came to Tarrant County in 1853 and established the Gibson community. Each brother donated land for this cemetery. The earliest marked grave belongs to Garrett Gibson's infant grandson who died in 1866. All but two of the seventy-three marked graves, many of which have only fieldstones, belong to relatives of the Gibson family.

Southlake

51. Absalom H. Chivers Cemetery, 1300 block of N. Carroll Avenue (marker is on private property, one-quarter mile west of N. Carroll Avenue and is not accessible by road)

Absalom H. Chivers, a prosperous farmer and stockman, came to Texas from Mississippi in 1852 and operated a farm along Dove Creek until his death in 1856. His grave is thought to be the earliest in this cemetery, which is located on his original homestead. His widow, Eleanor, set the land aside as a family cemetery in 1889. She died in 1896, and her grave is believed to be the last of the five graves placed in the cemetery.

52. Thomas Easter Cemetery, 2800 block of Southlake Boulevard

Virginia native Thomas Easter came to Texas about 1848 and settled on a 640-acre land grant in the northeast corner of Tarrant County. When he died in 1862, family members buried him here using a portion of his land holdings as a cemetery. Charity Easter, his wife, and Hardin West, both of whom died during the early 1880s, are also buried here. There are also a number of unmarked graves. The Easter Schoolhouse stood beside the burial ground during the nineteenth century.

53. Hood Cemetery, Coventry Lane at King's Court

Thomas Hood, a Peters colonist, came from Missouri about 1845 to farm this land. He and his second wife, Maryetta, are buried here in unmarked graves. Several other Peters colonists and Confederate veterans are also buried here. The earliest marked grave is that of Urias Martin, who died in 1855. In 1871, Hood's family formally set aside the one-acre cemetery tract. The cemetery is on privately owned land.

54. Lonesome Dove Baptist Church and Cemetery, 2380 Lonesome Dove Avenue

This church was organized in February 1846 in the home of Charles and Lucinda Throop by twenty-three Baptists. The first building at this site was erected in 1847, and the adjoining cemetery was organized in 1850. This historic site gave writer Larry McMurtry the name for his 1985 western epic and winner of the 1986 Pulitzer Prize, Lonesome Dove.

55. White's Chapel Cemetery, Southlake Boulevard at S. White's Chapel Road

According to local legend, this cemetery began about 1851, when a child traveling through this area in a wagon train died and was buried here. The oldest documented burial, that of infant Amy A. Marr, took place in 1872. Many graves in the pioneer cemetery are unmarked or are marked only with fieldstones. Native red sandstone is used for many of the markers and curbing.

Thematic Tours

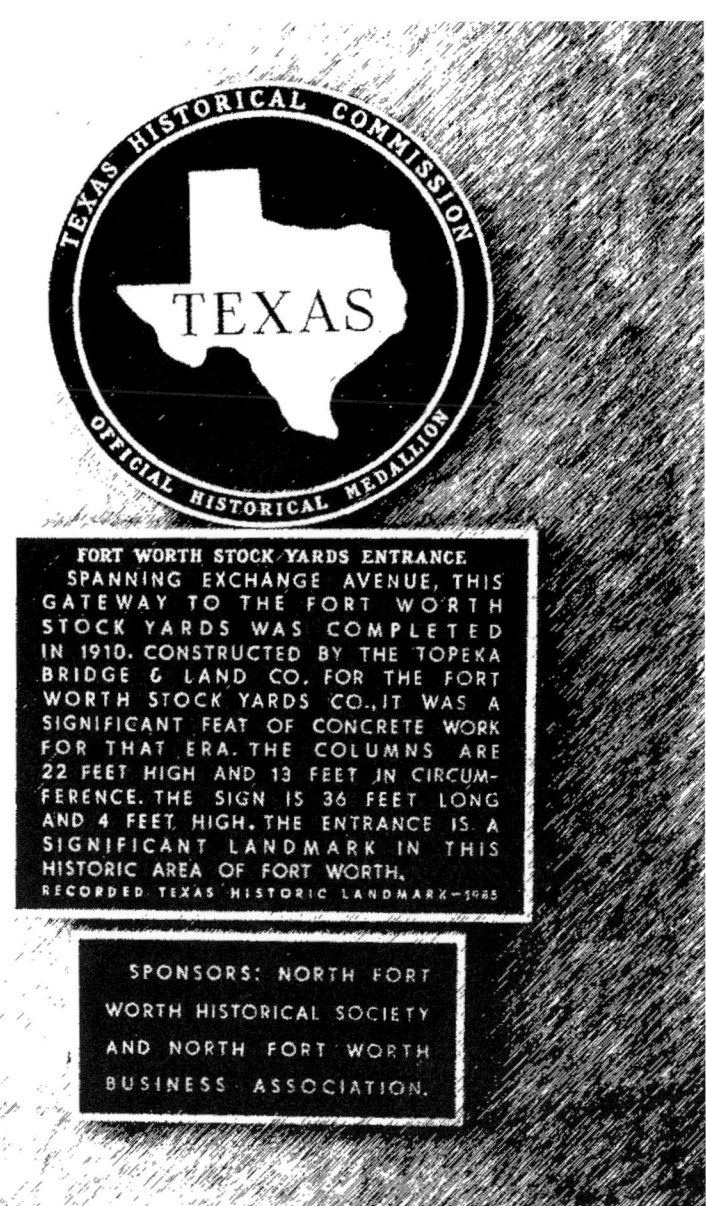

TEXAS HISTORICAL COMMISSION

TEXAS

OFFICIAL HISTORICAL MEDALLION

FORT WORTH STOCK YARDS ENTRANCE. SPANNING EXCHANGE AVENUE, THIS GATEWAY TO THE FORT WORTH STOCK YARDS WAS COMPLETED IN 1910. CONSTRUCTED BY THE TOPEKA BRIDGE & LAND CO. FOR THE FORT WORTH STOCK YARDS CO., IT WAS A SIGNIFICANT FEAT OF CONCRETE WORK FOR THAT ERA. THE COLUMNS ARE 22 FEET HIGH AND 13 FEET IN CIRCUM-FERENCE. THE SIGN IS 36 FEET LONG AND 4 FEET HIGH. THE ENTRANCE IS A SIGNIFICANT LANDMARK IN THIS HISTORIC AREA OF FORT WORTH.
RECORDED TEXAS HISTORIC LANDMARK—1985

SPONSORS: NORTH FORT WORTH HISTORICAL SOCIETY AND NORTH FORT WORTH BUSINESS ASSOCIATION.

African-American History

Fort Worth

Allen Chapel AME Church 32
Greater Saint James Baptist Church 32-33
Grand United Order of Odd Fellows Lodge 33-34
Morning Chapel CME Church 34
James E. Guinn School 67-68
I. M. Terrell High School 92
Riverside Public School 93
Mount Zion Baptist Church 93-94
Our Mother of Mercy Catholic Church and Parsonage 94
Near Southeast National Register Historic District 98-101
Oakwood Cemetery – William Madison McDonald grave 147

Arlington

Mount Olive Baptist Church 108

Azle

Smith-Frazier Cemetery 141

Haltom City

New Trinity Cemetery 151

Cattle and Livestock Industry

Burk Burnett Building   28
Hell's Half Acre   39-40
Fort Worth Stockyards National Register Historic District   47-55
Marine Commercial National Register Historic District   55-57
Grand Avenue National Register Historic District   57-58
Thistle Hill   65-66
Ball-Eddleman-McFarland House   80-81
Southwestern Exposition and Livestock Show   83-84

Early Tarrant County History

Fort Worth

Fort Worth: "Where the West Begins" marker   25

Van Zandt Cottage   82-83

Log Cabin Village   86

Ayres Cemetery   144

Pioneers Rest Cemetery   147

Arlington

Jopling-Melear Log Cabin   107

Marrow Bone Spring   107

Village Creek   108

Middleton Tate Johnson Plantation Cemetery and Park   139

Mansfield

Buchanan-Hayter-Witherspoon House   113

Man House   114

Haltom City

Birdville Cemetery   150

Grapevine

Torian Log Cabin   120

Minter's Chapel Cemetery   149

Keller

Mount Gilead Cemetery   152

Southlake

Lonesome Dove Church and Cemetery   154

Historic Residential Neigborhoods

Fort Worth
Grand Avenue National Register Historic District	57-58
Fairmount/Southside National Register Historic District	68-72
Elizabeth Boulevard National Register Historic District	72-75
Near Southeast National Register Historic District	98-101

Arlington
Old Town National Register Historic District	109-111

Grapevine
Original Town National Register Historic District	124-126

Jewish History

Marine Commercial National Register Historic District   56
Beth El Congregation   68
Congregation Ahavath Sholom   87
Ahavath Sholom Hebrew Cemetery   144
Emanuel Hebrew Rest Cemetery   146

Railroad History

Fort Worth
Texas & Pacific Railway Terminal and Inbound
    Freight Warehouse   41-42
Fort Worth Main Post Office   42
Santa Fe Depot   43
Fort Worth Stockyards National Register Historic
    District – Exchange Avenue Stairs   51
Central Handley National Register Historic District   96-98
Grapevine
Cotton Belt Railroad Industrial National Register
    Historic District   122-123

Acknowledgements

This revised edition of *Fort Worth and Tarrant County: An Historical Guide* continues a rich tradition that began in 1949 with the publication of *Down Historic Trails of Fort Worth and Tarrant County*, written by the Arlington Heights Junior Historians and edited by Dr. Julia Kathryn Garrett and Mary Daggett Lake. The second edition, *A Guide to Historic Sites in Fort Worth and Tarrant County* by W. J. Overton, was first published in 1963 and then revised, expanded, and reprinted four times. In 1984, Ruby Schmidt continued the tradition with *Fort Worth and Tarrant County: A Historical Guide*. All editions of this pocket guide to Tarrant County history have had the support of the Tarrant County Historical Society, Inc., a tradition that continues with this new version. I am grateful to the Tarrant County Historical Society, Inc., for all they have done to preserve Tarrant County history, for their suggestions about this book, and for their financial support of this project. In particular, Joyce Pate Capper, past-president, and Robert Capper, president, have been strong backers of this endeavor.

Tarrant County historians have substantially expanded the body of knowledge covering the area's history in the almost twenty years since the last edition of this work was published. The scope of historical research has broadened beyond the pioneer endeavors of the nineteenth century and the early years of the twentieth century to include a wider variety of people, places, and events. As with Ruby Schmidt's edition, this guide includes buildings, historic districts, and sites that have been listed in the National Register of Historic Places or received a Texas Historical

Marker. The research undertaken to document these historic resources has provided a wealth of information for this book. The Texas Historical Commission has made much of this information available on the Internet through the Texas Historic Sites Atlas (http://atlas.thc.state.tx.us/), which allows searches by the type of historical designation, by county, or by the name of a property. I am grateful to the Texas Historical Commission for allowing me to use information from these files for this book.

I also want to thank Ruby Schmidt for her wisdom and guidance, Diane Williams for her information about properties in Mansfield, and Judy George-Garza and Michelle Mears of the Texas Historical Commission for providing copies of nominations not available through the Texas Historic Sites Atlas. Judy Alter, director of the TCU Press, is both a friend and a colleague, and I respect and appreciate the guidance she gave in shaping the content of this guide. I also want to thank my husband, Lon, my family, and my colleagues at the Dallas Public Library for their support and encouragement.

Carol Roark
May 2, 2003

Index

A

African Americans, 10, 23, 32-34, 92-94, 98-101, 141
Agriculture, 6, 113, 119
Ahavath Sholom Hebrew Cemetery, 144, 162
Akron plan, 30
Alcon Laboratories, Inc., 8
Allen Chapel African Methodist Episcopal Church, 32, 158
Allen, Permelia, 152
Alliance Airport, 8
American Airlines, 13
Amon Carter Museum, 13
Amon G. Carter Field, 8
Amtrak, 43
Anderson, Neil P., Building, 35-36
Arlington, 4, 7, 103-111, 138-140
Arlington Cemetery, 140
Arlington Heights, 12, 79, 84-86
Arlington Heights Lodge #1184 A. F. & A. M., 84
Arlington Post Office, 105-106
Armour & Company Packing and Provision Plant, 4-5, 11, 25, 47, 48, 50, 51-52
Armour & Swift Plaza, 51
Armstrong and Messer, architectural firm, 41
Armstrong House, 58
Armstrong, William L., 58
Army, United States, 5
Arnold, Major Ripley A., 2, 10, 25, 147
Arwine Cemetery, 151
Arwine, Daniel, 151
Arwine, Katy, 151
Ash Creek Cemetery, 141
Athol, 10
Austin, Stephen F., Elementary School, 64-65

Austral windows, 36
Autrey, William, 141
Aviation industry, 7-8, 13, 119-120, 131
Ayres, Benjamin Patton, 144
Ayres Cemetery, 144, 160
Azle, 2, 6, 11, 141
Azle Cemetery Association, 141

B

B & D Mills, 123
Ball-Eddleman-McFarland House, 80-81, 159
Ball, Sarah C., 80
Bancroft, Daniel, 152
Barkley, Benjamin Franklin, 150
Barron Field, 5
Baseball teams, 6
Bass, Nancy Lee and Perry R., Performance Hall, 14
Bass, Sam, 40
Battle of Village Creek, 10, 108
Bear Creek Cemetery, 143
Bear Creek Missionary Baptist Church, 143
Bedford, 10, 126-127, 141
Bedford Cemetery, 141
Bedford College, 126
Bedford School, 126-127
Bell Helicopter Textron, Inc., 7-8
Benbrook, 5-6, 148
Benbrook Field, 5
Benbrook, James M., 148
Benton House, 69-70
Benton, Ella Belle and Meredith, 70
Berachah Home and Cemetery, 138
Berachah Rescue Society, 138
Berney, Morris, 35
Beth-El Congregation, 68, 146, 162
Bidault, Anthelm, 119
Bidault House, 119
Biggs, Electra Waggoner, 84
Bird, Jonathan, 10, 150

Bird's Fort, 10, 150
Bird's Fort, Treaty of, 2, 10, 107, 108
Birdville, 2, 10, 13, 150
Birdville Cemetery, 150, 160
Blackstone Hotel, 6, 29
Blackwell, Hiram, 107
Bobo, Bettie W., 141
Bobo, Weldon W., 10, 126
Boon, J. D., 94
Bourland, Aurelius Delphus, 152
Bourland Cemetery, 152
Bowlin, Mattic C. and James W., 148
Bowman, Euday Louis, 147
Bratton, Emma and Andrew, 113-114
Bratton House, 113-114
Breckenridge, 5
Brenneke and Fay, engineers, 26
Brooks, Dr. W. B., 10
Bryce Building, 38
Bryce Building Company, 38
Bryce House, 84-85
Bryce, William J., 38, 84-85
Buchanan and Gilder, contractors, 28
Buchanan-Hayter-Witherspoon House,
    113, 160
Buchanan, Thomas and R. A., 113
Buck Oaks Farm, 131
Buck, Katherine and Raymond E., 131
Bunch, Eugene, 40
Bureau of Printing and Engraving, 14
Burgee, John, 40
Burk Burnett Building, 28, 159
Burkburnett, 5
Burke Cemetery, 145
Burke, Mary Overton, 145
Burlington Northern Santa Fe Railway, 8
Burnett, Ethelyn and Jesse, 100
Burnett House, 100
Burnett Park, 35, 37
Burnett, Samuel Burk, 28, 147
Burts, Dr. W. P., 10
Butler, H. H., 10
Byrne & Luther, Inc., 132

C

Calloway, Catherine and Richard H., 143
Calloway Cemetery, 143
Calloway, Joseph W., 143
Calvary Cemetery, 147
Cameron, R. A., 40
Camp Bowie, 5-6, 12, 40, 84, 119
Capps, William, 81
Carruthers Field, 5, 12
Carswell Air Force Base, 7, 12, 14, 131
Carter, Amon G., 7, 84
Caruso, Enrico, 49
Casa Mañana, 12-13
Cassidy, Butch, 40
Castle, Vernon, 12
Cate, James 149
Cattle drives, 3, 25
Cattle industry, 3-5, 25, 28, 31, 36, 42,
    47-55, 65-66, 80-81, 159
Central Handley National Register
    Historic District, 96-98, 163
Chamberlain Development Company, 79
Chapel Cemetery, 145
Chase Court, 68
Chicago, Rock Island & Gulf Railway,
    11, 126
Chisholm Trail, 25
Chivers, Absalom H., Cemetery, 153
Chivers, Eleanor, 153
Citizens Hotel Company, 31
City Beautiful Movement, 72
Civil Courts Building, 24
Civil War, 2-3
Civilian Conservation Corps, 6
Clarkson, Wiley G., 28, 31, 36, 67, 73,
    74, 80, 95
Clements Cemetery, 149
Coble, Allen B., 148
Coble, Samuel D., 148
Coliseum, 48-49
Colleyville, 6, 13, 119, 141-142
Colley, Dr. Lilburn Howard, 13, 119

Colonial National Invitational Golf Tournament, 12

Como Weekly, 12

Congregation Ahavath Sholom, 87, 146, 162

Consolidated Vultee Aircraft Corporation, 7, 12

Cook Children's Medical Center, 8

Cooper, Mattie Luna, 138

Corinth Baptist Church, 93

Cotton Belt Depot, 122-123

Cotton Belt Railroad Industrial National Register Historic District, 122-123, 163

Cotton Belt Route, 11, 119, 122-123

Courtyard by Marriott Downtown-Blackstone, 29

Cowtown, 25, 47

Cret, Paul Philippe, 36

Cross Timbers, 2, 86

Cross Timbers Trading Post No. 1, 107

Crowley, 10, 142

Crowley, Isham, 143

Crowley, Joe O., 109

Crowley, S. H., 10

Cultural District, 7, 79

Cumberland Presbyterian Cemetery, 153

Cumberland Presbyterian Church, 153

Curtis, Victor Marr, 132

D

Daggett, Charles B., 146

Daggett, Ephraim M., 147

Dallas-Fort Worth International Airport, 8, 13, 119, 120, 126, 143, 149

Dallas-Fort Worth Turnpike, 7, 13, 140

Darnall, Emma, 69

Darnall House, 69

Daughters of the Republic of Texas, 83

Davies, J. C., 84

Dean, A. M., 30

Deer Creek, 10, 142

Deer Creek Cemetery, 142

Defense industry, 7, 12, 14, 131

Denis, Father Narcissus P., 94

Desdemona, 5

Dido, 142

Dido Cemetery, 142

Dobkins, Alexander, Family Cemetery, 143

Dobkins, Mary and Alexander, 143

Dorris House, 124

Dorris, Dr. Thomas Benton, 124

Dove, 120

Dozier, Otis, 106

Douglass, Clara and Wilson M., 110

Douglass-Potts House, 109-110

Driskell, Christina, 149

Dulaney House, 72-73

Dulaney, Richard O., 28, 72-73

Dunn, Sarah J., 142

E

Earp, Wyatt, 40

East Fort Worth Town Company, 91

Easter, Charity, 154

Easter Schoolhouse, 154

Easter, Thomas, Cemetery, 153-154

Eddleman-McFarland House, 80-81

Eddleman, William H., 80

Edelman, Samuel, 69

Edlebrock Commercial Building, 54

Electric Building, 35

Elizabeth Boulevard National Register Historic District, 72-75, 161

Emanuel Hebrew Rest Cemetery, 146, 162

Enon, 143

Estill, Frank and Charles, 124, 127

Euless, 13, 143

Euless, Elisha Adam, 13

Everman, 5-6, 11, 143-144

Everman Cemetery, 143-144

Everman, John W., 143

Exchange Avenue Stairs, 51

F

Fairmount/Southside National Register
Historic District, 68-72, 161
Fairview/Bryce House, 84-85
Fanning, John, 145
Farmer, Elijah, 131
Farmer, Jane and Press, 144
Farmers & Merchants Milling Company,
123, 126
Farrell, John E., 133
Farrington Field, 6
Farris, Hiram Jackson, 143
Feild, Julian, 42, 113, 114
Field and Clarkson, architectural firm,
74
Field, E. S., 74, 147
Fielder House, 106
Fielder, Mattie and James Park, 106
Fielder Museum, 106
Fincher's White Front Store, 52-53
First Christian Church, 30, 144
Flatiron Building, 37-38
Ford Cemetery, 148
Ford, Pinkney Harold, 148
Forest Hill, 144
Forest Hill Cemetery, 144
Fort Worth
annexation, 55, 57, 91-92
cemeteries, 144-148
military fort, 2, 25, 26
rivalry with Dallas, 3, 8-9
schools, 6, 39, 64-65, 67-68, 92-93, 95-
96
Fort Worth Art Museum, 13
Fort Worth Botanic Garden, 81-82
Fort Worth Business Assistance Center,
68
Fort Worth Cats, 6
Fort Worth Convention Center, 40
Fort Worth Cotton and Grain Exchange,
35
Fort Worth Extension Company, 132

Fort Worth Frontier Centennial, 7, 12,
79
Fort Worth Garden Club, 81-82
Fort Worth Laundry Company, 55
Fort Worth Live Stock Exchange, 49
Fort Worth Main Post Office, 42, 163
Fort Worth Power and Light Company,
35
Fort Worth Public Library, 11, 38
Fort Worth Star-Telegram, 11, 132
Fort Worth Stock Yards Company, 48-50,
52
Fort Worth Stock Yards Sign, 48
Fort Worth Stockyards National Register
Historic District, 47-55, 159, 163
Fort Worth Union Depot, 43
Fort Worth Water Garden, 13, 39-40
Frank Leslie's Illustrated Newspaper, 41
Fretwell, Rev. Greene, 151
Friday House, 106-107
Friday, Marion and Willie Maybelle, 106-
107
Fuller-Snyder House, 75
Fuller, William Marshall, 75

G

General Motors Assembly Plant, 7, 105
Gibbins, Amanda and Thomas, 138
Gibbins Cemetery and Homestead Site,
138
Gibbins, James, 138
Gibbins, Martha H., 138
Gibson, 153
Gibson Cemetery, 153
Gibson, Garrett, 153
Gibson, James, 153
Girl's Service League, 66
Glasgow, Earl T., 131
Globe Aircraft Corporation, 7
Goldsmith, John Alison, 141
Goldstein, William, 87
Goodwin, John J., 148

Goodwin, Mrs. Micajah, 140

Gouhenant, Adolphus, 147

Grand Avenue National Register
Historic District, 57-58, 159, 161

Grand Prairie, 2, 148

Grand United Order of Odd Fellows,
Lodge No. 2144, 33-34, 158

Grapevine, 2, 4, 9, 11, 119-126, 148-149

Grapevine Cemetery, 148-149

Grapevine Commercial National Register
Historic District, 120-122

Grapevine Heritage Foundation, 123

Grapevine Historical Society, 123

Grapevine Home Bank, 121

Grapevine Sun, 121, 126

Grapevine Vintage Railroad, 123

Great Depression, 6, 41-42, 82, 106, 152

Greater Saint James Baptist Church, 32-
33, 158

Greater Southwest International Airport,
8

Greenwood Cemetery Association, 144

Gregg, W. P., 141

Greines Furniture Company, 56

Greines, Meyer, 56

Grubbs Vocational College, 111

Guinn, Dr. Edward, 13

Guinn, James E., 67

Guinn, James E., School, 67-68, 158

Guiry, Louisa C., 149

Gulf Oil, 5

Gunn and Curtiss, architectural firm, 24

H

Haggart and Sanguinet, architectural
firm, 28

Hall, A. S., 94

Hall, Marjorie and Lee, 115

Hall, W. D., 94

Haltom City, 10, 13, 150-151

Handley, 91-92, 96-98

Handley Cemetery, 139

Handley Feed Store, 97

Handley, James M., 96, 139

Handley Post Office, 98

Handley Power Plant, 96

Harden, John J., 64

Hare, S. Herbert, 82

Harper, Henry Jackson, 150-151

Harper, Mary Jane, 151

Harper's Rest Cemetery, 150-151

Harrington, Ryan, 142

Harrison Cemetery, 146

Harrison, D. C., 146

Harrison, Mary, 146

Hart, J. H., 115

Harris Methodist Hospitals, 8

Hayne, Alfred S., 41

Hayne, Al, Monument, 40-41

Hedrick, Wyatt C., 35, 41, 42, 67

Hell's Half Acre, 39-40, 159

Heritage Park, 123

Hicks Field, 5

Hill, The, 108

Hillside Apartments, 32

Hilton Hotel, 29

Historic Fort Worth, Inc., 81

Hitch Cemetery, 146

Hitch, William Henry, 146

Hoffer-Hulen House, 73-74

Hoffer, Temple B., 73-74

Hog & Sheep Pens, 50-51

Hollywood Theatre, 35

Holy Name Catholic Church, 99

Holt, Dempsy S., 142

Home for Aged Masons, 95

Hood Cemetery, 154

Hood, Maryetta and Thomas, 154

Horse & Mule Barns, 50

Hotel Texas, 6, 13, 31

Hubbard Drug Store, 97

Hudson, Ary Mae and Arra Bell, 152

Hudson Cemetery, 152

Huffman House, 70-71

Huffman, James B., 70-71

Hulen, Major General John A., 74
Hurwitz, Charles, 144
Hurst, 6, 151-152
Hurst, William Letchworth, 11, 141
Hutcheson, I. L., 109
Hutcheson-Smith House, 109
Hutcheson, William T., 109

I

International & Great Northern
    Railroad, 11
Interstate 30, 7, 64
Interstate 35W, 7
Interurban, 11-12, 91, 96, 105, 107, 111, 126

J

James, Harry, 49
Jarvis, J. J., 141
Jary, William E., 57
Johnson, Middleton Tate, 107
Johnson, Philip, 40
Johnson Plantation Cemetery, 9, 107,
    139, 160
Johnson Station, 2, 107, 139
Jopling, George Washington, 107
Jopling-Melear Log Cabin, 107, 160
Jordan-Edelman House, 69
Josephites, 94
Joyce, William, 152

K

Kaiser, Leah, 146
Keller, 6, 10, 152
Keller, John C., 10
Kennedale, 152-153
Kennedy, John F., 13, 31
Kerr, Zenas Ewin, 146
Kessler, George, 81-82
Kimbell Art Museum, 13
Knights of Pythias Castle Hall, 27

Koeppe, Earl, 41-42
Kornbleet Chapel, 144

L

La Cava Cleaners, 71
La Reunion Colony, 119
Lake Arlington, 96, 108
Lake Erie, 96
Lake Grapevine, 13
Lake, Mary Daggett, 81-82
Lake Worth, 6, 12
Lancaster Crowley Properties, 98
Lancaster, John L., 41
Land Title Block, 27-28
La Salle, Rene Robert Cavelier, Sieur de,
    107
Leftover Hills, 132
Levy, Sam, 68
Liberation Community, Inc., 107
Live Stock Exchange, 49-50
Lockheed Martin, 7-8, 12
Lockheed Martin Recreation Area, 145
Log cabins, 86, 107, 114, 120
Log Cabin Village, 9, 86, 152, 160
Lonesome Dove, 154
Lonesome Dove Baptist Church and
    Cemetery, 154, 160
Lucas Grocery, 121-122

M

Magnolia Petroleum, 5
Man House, 114, 160
Man, Julia Boisseau, 114, 153
Man, Ralph Sandiford, 113, 114
Mansfield, 4, 10-11, 113, 115, 153
Mansfield Male and Female College, 10,
    115
Marinda, 148
Marine, 55
Marine Commercial National Register
    Historic District, 55-57, 159, 162

Marine Creek, 11, 48, 53, 55

Marine Theater, 56-57

Marr, Amy A., 154

Marrow Bone Spring, 107, 160

Martin-Campbell House, 70

Martin, Julia, 70

Martin, Urias, 154

Masonic Cemetery, 138

Masonic Temple, 79-80

Masonic Widows and Orphans Home National Register Historic District, 95-96

Masterson, Bat, 40

Mayton, Henry, 151

McDonald, William Madison, 98, 147

McFarland, Caroline and Frank H., 81

McMurtry, Larry, 154

McNatt, William, Cemetery, 128

McPeak, Flavius G., 146

Mechau, Frank A., Jr., 37

Meacham Field, 6, 12

Meador, W. C., 34

Meadowbrook, 91

Meatpacking industry, 4-5, 13, 37-38, 47-52

Melear, Jane Catherine and Z. T., 107

Messer, Howard, 80

Messer, Sanguinet and Messer, architectural firm, 64, 84

Mexican Americans, 56-57

Middleton Tate Johnson Plantation Cemetery and Park, 9, 107, 139, 160

Midway Airport, 8

Miller, Mary, 139

Mineral water well, 107

Minter, Green W., 149

Minter's Chapel Cemetery, 149, 160

Minter's Chapel Methodist Church, 149

Mitchell, James E., 65

Mitchell-Schoonover House, 65

Modern Drug, 71

Molly, stockyards symbol, 49

Monticello, 6

Moore, Milton, 141

Moorehead, James Tracy, 149

Morgan Hood Survey Pioneer Cemetery, 149

Morning Chapel C. M. E. Church, 34, 158

Morningside, 91

Morris Graveyard, 144

Morris, Rosa and R. E., 143

Morrow, Robert, 121

Morrison, Dave, 141

Mosier Valley, 10

Mount Gilead Baptist Church, 32

Mount Gilead Cemetery, 152, 160

Mount Olive Baptist Church, 108, 158

Mount Olivet Cemetery, 146-147

Mount Olivet Cemetery Association, 145

Mount Zion Baptist Church, 93-94, 101, 158

Mule Alley, 50

Mulholland Company, 56

Munchus, Dr. George M., 100

Munchus House, 100

Mural paintings, 37, 106

N

Naval Air Station/Joint Reserve Base/Fort Worth Carswell Field, 12, 14, 131

Navarro County, 10

Neace, Iraneous, 152

Near Southeast National Register Historic District, 98-101, 158, 161

Negro Community Hospital, 100

New Isis Theater, 54-55

New Trinity Cemetery, 151, 158

Newby, Etta (Mrs. William G.), 66

Newton, A. M., 149

Nicolais, Raphael A., 73

Niles City, 12

Nokia, 8

North Fort Worth, 55, 57
North Fort Worth Historical Society, museum, 49
Northern Texas Traction Company, 96
Nugent, Christina and Joseph, 115
Nugent-Hart House, 115

O

Oakhurst, 91
Oakwood Cemetery and Chapel, 147, 158
O'Bar, 11
O'Bar, William, 11
Odd Fellows Lodge, 33-34, 100
O'Keefe, C. A., 29
Old City Cemetery, Arlington, 138
Old Town National Register Historic District, Arlington, 109-111, 161
Oneal-Sells Administration Building, TWU, 94-95
Original Town National Register Historic District, Grapevine, 124-126, 161
Our Mother of Mercy Catholic Church, 94, 99, 158

P

Paddock, B. B., 4, 26
Paddock Viaduct, 26
Panther City, 3, 38
Parker Cabin, 86, 151-152
Parker Cemetery, 151-152
Parker, Cynthia Ann, 86, 151
Parker, Isaac Duke, 86, 151-152
Parker, Isaac Green, 149
Parker Memorial Cemetery, 149
Pate Museum of Transportation, 43
Patterson, L. G., 153
Peace, Joe, 34
Peak, Carroll M., 147
People's Burial Park, 151

Peters Colony, 10, 107, 120, 143, 148, 149, 152, 154
Petroleum industry, 5-6, 12
Pierce Oil, 5
Pioneers Rest Cemetery, 147, 160
Pittman, William Sidney, 32
Pleasant Glade, 149
Pollock-Capps House, 81
Pollock, Joseph R., 81
Polytechnic College, 91, 94
Polytechnic Heights, 12, 91, 94
Post Offices, 42, 98, 106
Potts, Clara and W. A., 110g
Potts, Wiley Wilda, 150
Powell, George, 33
Presley, Elvis, 49
Prince, Allen, 141
Prohibition, 12
Prostitution, 3, 39-40, 138
Pryor, Rev. A. W., 101
Pryor House, 101
Pulley House, 110
Pulley, Nannie and W. J., 110
Public Market Building, 64
Public Works Administration, 6
Purity Journal, 138

Q

Quality Hill, 80-81

R

Radio Shack, 8
Radisson Plaza Fort Worth, 31
Raibourn, Eliny, 145
Railroad industry, 3-4, 8, 41-43, 96-98, 122-123, 143-144
Randol Mill, 146
Randol, R. A., 146
Ranger, 5
Red River Crossing, 25
Reeves-Walker House, 71-72

Reeves, William, 71
Rehoboth Baptist Church, 139
Rehoboth Cemetery, 139
Rhodes, B. G., 33
Riley Cemetery, 141
Riley, Jonathan, 141
Riley, Thomas, 141
River Legacy Parks, 138
Rivercrest, 6
Riverside, 12, 91
Riverside Public School, 93, 158
Robinson, Charles H., 100
Robinson, Elizabeth, 139
Robinson, Rev. J. Francis, 32
Rodeos, 47, 48, 83
Rodgers Cemetery, 152-153
Rodgers, Mary and Thomas, 152
Rogers, Will, 84
Rolla, Lenora, 13
Roosevelt, Theodore, 11
Rose/Roseland/Marine Theater, 56-57
Rose Hill Cemetery, 139
Ross Brothers Horse and Mule Company, 58
Ross, Head and Ross, law firm, 28
Ross, Waddy R., 58
Ryan, John C., 72, 73, 74
Ryan Place, 6, 72
Ryan-Smith House, 74

S

Saginaw, 5-7, 11
Saint Ignatius Academy, 39
Saint Joseph Society of the Sacred Heart, 94
Saint Louis and Southwestern Railway, 11, 119
Saint Louis, Arkansas and Texas Railway, 11, 119
Saint Mary of the Assumption Catholic Church, 67
Saint Patrick Cathedral, 38-39
Samuel, Baldwin L., 147
Sanguinet and Staats, architectural firm, 26, 28, 31, 36, 37, 65, 85, 125
Sanguinet House, 85-86
Sanguinet, Marshall R., 26, 27-28, 31, 36, 37, 64, 65, 67, 85-86, 125
Sanguinet, Staats and Hedrick, architectural firm, 67
Santa Fe Depot, 43, 163
Saunders, Dr. Bacon, 37
Save-the-Scott-Home, 66
Schools, 6, 10-11, 39, 64-65, 67-68, 92-93, 95-96, 126, 139, 148
Schoonover, Maurine and Frank, 65
Scoggins, Sarah M. and George, 82
Scott, Elizabeth, 65
Scott, Winfield, 65, 147
Scott, Winfield, Jr., 65-66
Sears Roebuck & Company, 119
Sexton, Enoch, 151
Shelton, Anna, 66
Short, Luke, 40, 147
Simmons, Charles B., 65
Simon, Louis A., 105
Sinclair Building, 28-29
Singleton, Frank J., 33, 125
Sisters of Saint Mary of Namur, 39
Sixth Ward School, 64
Smith, Bert K., 74
Smith-Frazier Cemetery, 141, 158
Smith House, 74-75
Smith, John Peter, 146, 147
Smith, Jule G., 74
Smith, S. T., 109
Snyder, Marinda Willburn, 148
Snyder, Susie and D. H., 75
South Side Colored School, 67
Southlake, 153-154
Southwestern Baptist Theological Seminary, 11
Southwestern Exposition and Fat Stock Show, 28

Southwestern Exposition and Livestock Show, 79, 83-84, 159
Sparks House, 73
Sparks, John, 73
Spring Palace, 11, 40-41
Squires, Rev. 108
Staats, Carl, 85
Starr, Barton H., 149
Stephens, Lemuel, 115
Stephenson, Thomas D., 142
Stevens, O. D., Commercial Building, 97
Stevens, Orley D., 97
Steward, Dr. James Azle, 11, 141
Stewart, Clarence, 124
Stewart House, 124
Stock show, 11, 28, 48, 79, 83-84, 159
Stock Yards Club Saloon, 43
Stock Yards Lodge No. 1244, 54
Stock Yards National Bank, 52-53, 73
Stockyards, 47-55
Stockyards Hotel, 53-54
Stockyards Station, 50-51
Stop Six, 91
Strategic Air Command, 7
Streetcars, 51, 64, 68, 79, 91
Sublett, 139
Sublett, John, 139
Sundance Kid, 40
Sundance Square, 9, 13
Sunday, Billy, 49
Sunshine Presbyterian Church, 94
Sweet Chapel Cemetery, 145
Sweet Chapel Methodist Church, 145
Swift & Co., 4-5, 11, 13, 25, 47, 48, 50, 51, 52
Swift & Co. General Office Building, 52
Swift & Co. Meatpacking Plant, 52

T

Taliaferro Fields #1, #2, and #3, 5
Tandy, George E., 94
Tarrant County, established, 10

Tarrant County Black Historical and Genealogical Society, 13
Tarrant County Courthouse, 11, 24
Tarrant County Criminal Courts Building, 26
Tarrant County State Bank Building, 121
Tarrant Field Aerodrome, 12
Tarrant, General Edward H., 2, 108, 147
Tate Cemetery, 140
Tate, E. C., 140
Tate Springs, 140
Taylor, Elmer L., 111
Taylor House, 111
Terrell, I. M., High School, 92, 158
Terrell, Isaiah Milligan, 92
Texas & Pacific Railway, 2, 10, 40, 41-42, 63, 97, 105
Texas & Pacific Railway Inbound Freight Warehouse, 41-42, 163
Texas & Pacific Railway Terminal, 41-42, 163
Texas and Southwestern Cattle Raisers Association, 28, 31
Texas Centennial, 83
Texas Christian University, 11
Texas Electric Service Company, 96
Texas League baseball, 6
Texas Log Cabins, 86
Texas Sesquicentennial, 13
Texas Spring Palace, 11, 40-41
Texas State Teachers Association Building, 31
Texas Wesleyan University, 91, 94-95
Thannisch Block, 53-54
Thannisch, Thomas M., 53
The Hill, 108
Thistle Hill, 65-66, 159
Thomas, Jane E., 139
Throop, Francis, 120
Throop, Lucinda and Charles, 154
Thurmond, Amanda, 142
Thurmond, Dave, 142
Tomkins Log Cabin, 86

Tomlin Cemetery, 140
Tomlin, James Tives, 140
Tomlin, Soloman, 140
Torian, John R., 120
Torian Log Cabin, 120, 160
Trayler, Maria, 148
Treaty of Bird's Fort, 2, 10, 107, 108
Tribune, Frank, 93-94
Trinity Cemetery, 147
Trinity Chapel Methodist Church, 151
Trinity Railway Express, 14, 42
Trinity River, 2, 26, 79, 108
Turnpike, 7

U

Union Stockyards Co., 4
United Daughters of the Confederacy,
   83, 147
United States Army, 5
United States Courthouse, 36-37
United States Department of
   Agriculture, 35
United States Highway, 81
United States Treasury Section of Fine
   Arts program, 37, 106
University of Texas at Arlington, 105,
   111
Upchurch, Rev. James T., 138

V

Van Cliburn International Piano
   Competition, 13
Van Slyke, E. W., 30
Van Zandt Cottage, 82-83, 160
Van Zandt Farm, 79
Van Zandt, Dr. Isaac L., 142
Van Zandt, Major K. M., 30, 82
Van Zandt, Townes, 142
Village Creek, 10, 108, 160

W

Waggoner, Electra, 65
Waggoner, W. T., 36, 65, 147
Waggoner, W. T., Building, 36
Wall House, 125-126
Wall, Benjamin R., 125
Walker, Myrtle and John, 71
Wallace-Hall House, 115
Wallace, Mary Ann and James, 115
Waller, Marion L., 94, 147
Washington, Booker T., 32
Water Garden, 13, 39-40
Watson, 140
Watson Cabin, 107, 140
Watson, Jack D., Post Office, 42
Watson, P. A., Cemetery, 140
Watson, Patrick Alfred, 140
WBAP Radio, 12, 29
WBAP Television, 12
Weiler House, 98
Weiler, Rose and William, 98
West, Hardin, 154
Western Currency Facility, 14
Western Heights Missionary Baptist
   Church, 143
Westover Hills, 132-133
Westover Manor, 132-133
Westworth Village, 131
Whalen, Joseph L., 57
Whalen-Jary House, 57
Wharton, Albert B., 65
Wharton-Scott House, 65-66
Where the West Begins, 2, 8, 25, 160
White, A. Delphus, 152
White's Chapel Cemetery, 154
Wiese, Allie Mae and Frank, 138
Wiggins House, 124, 125
Wiggins, Mary Lipscomb, 125
Will Rogers Memorial Coliseum and
   Auditorium, 6
Willburn Cemetery, 148
Willburn, Cassandra and William, 148

Willburn, Nancy and Edward, 148
Williams, Eunice, 138
Williamson-Dickie Manufacturing
    Company, 64-65
Wilson Cemetery, 148
Wilson, Charles N., 148
Withers, Elmer G., architectural
    company, 67
Witten Cemetery, 142
Witten, Samuel Cecil Holiday, 142
Witten, William Cecil, 141
Woman's Club Buildings, 66
Women in Construction, Fort Worth
    Chapter, 147
Women's Humane Association, 41
Woodruff, Clyde, 30
Works Progress Administration, 152
World War I, 5, 40, 74
World War II, 7
Worth, Major William Jenkins, 25
Worthington National Bank, 105-106

Y

Young, Charles, 141

About the Author

Carol Roark is manager of the Special Collections division at the Dallas Public Library. This department includes the Texas/Dallas History and Archives Division and Fine Books. Carol has a Masters degree in American Studies (an interdisciplinary program involving history, art history, and literature) from Texas Christian University and a Masters in Library Science from the University of North Texas. Prior to joining the staff of the Dallas Public Library in 1991, she worked in the Amon Carter Museum's photography collection and with the Historic Preservation Council for Tarrant County, where she edited and published four volumes of the *Tarrant County Historic Resources Survey*. The survey books list and give a brief history of over 2,200 architecturally and historically significant structures in Fort Worth and Tarrant County.

Carol lives in an historic neighborhood, where she and her husband have renovated a 1913 bungalow. She is chair of the Texas Historical Commission's National Register State Board of Review, which evaluates buildings that have been nominated to the National Register of Historic Places. Her books include *Fort Worth's Legendary Landmarks*, a volume that highlights eighty of Fort Worth's most important historic buildings, and *Fort Worth Then & Now*, which pairs historic and contemporary photographs of the same place or event.